TRADITIONAL
MUSIC
OF
AMERICA

Da Capo Press Music Reprint Series

MUSIC EDITOR
BEA FRIEDLAND
Ph.D., City University of New York

TRADITIONAL MUSIC OF AMERICA

Ira W. Ford

Introduction by
JUDITH McCULLOH

DA CAPO PRESS • NEW YORK • 1978

Library of Congress Cataloging in Publication Data

Ford, Ira W
  Traditional music of America.

  (Da Capo Press music reprint series)
  Principally fiddle tunes, in part with words.
  Reprint of the 1st ed. published by E. P. Dutton,
New York.
  1. Folk music, American. 2. Folk-songs, American.
3. Ballads, American. 4. Fiddle tunes. I. Title.
[M1629.F69T7 1978]   781.7'73   78-2026
ISBN 0-306-77588-3

Reprinted from the original edition of 1940 by arrangement with
E. P. Dutton & Co., Inc., and including the new introduction published in a 1965 reprint, with the permission of Judith McCulloh.

Published by Da Capo Press, Inc.
A Subsidiary of Plenum Publishing Corporation
227 West 17th Street, New York, N.Y. 10011

1-10-79

INTRODUCTION

In 1940 two important and complementary collections of folk music appeared: *Ballads and Songs Collected by the Missouri Folk-Lore Society*, edited by Henry M. Belden, and Traditional Music of America, compiled and edited by Ira W. Ford. The Belden work is comprised of song texts, with tunes appended as they could be secured. One of a number of state collections representative of scholarly activity in the earlier years of this century, the collection expressly presents Missouri folksong. Documentation of the individual items, prepared by a professor of English and one of the most active and alert folklorists of his day, remains exemplary; the immediate source of each item is given, and, with the data available at that time, each is identified as to provenance and distribution.

By contrast, Ira Ford's preoccupation was with instrumental music, above all with old-time fiddle tunes. Song texts, snatches of verse, tune legends, "Americana" were all important, but added. Where the arrangement in Belden's collection was Child-and-other, in Ford's it was fiddle tune-and-other. While the title Traditional Music of America claimed national coverage, we infer from internal evidence and from the known facts of Ford's life that the bulk of his material represents Missouri tradition.

The chief problem with this collection is that for any given item we cannot with certainty answer the core questions Who? When? Where?, let alone How? and Why? Edward H. Weatherly, in his foreword to the 1955 reprint edition of Belden's *Ballads and Songs*, had justly labeled it "a pioneer work" (ix). Traditional Music of America was also a pioneer work, but of a different color. Ford, "a descendant of American pioneers," wrote to the original publisher, E. P. Dutton (New York), that his purpose in writing the book was "to preserve and revive, for this mighty nation, some of the lore bequeathed to us by our mighty pioneers." The frontier was not static, and Ford saw no need to pinpoint tunes and persons as they appeared in pioneer history. The frontier was not confined to Missouri, but moved over the nation, and Ford, in full patriotic energy, chose to honor the whole rather than the part.

Ford falls within several of the categories discussed by D. K. Wilgus in *Anglo-American Folksong Scholarship Since 1898* (New Brunswick, New Jersey, 1959): local-enthusiast, musical-esthetic, amateur collector (see 156ff., 167ff., 181ff.). But he seems to have worked in singular isolation from the academic community, even from other local collectors, and I doubt he was ever aware that he partook of this larger tradition.

It is also an unhappy fact that the academic community remained virtually unaware of Ford during his lifetime. The first scholarly review of TRADITIONAL MUSIC OF AMERICA was negative, almost indignant; Herbert Halpert wrote in the *Journal of American Folklore* (Vol. 54, 1941):

> This is obviously a fine gift book, a well-made volume with good paper, clearly set music and excellent print, but the recipient must remember the saying about gift horses . . . The compiler of this collection (the title is superb arrogance) views himself as a pioneer in the field of traditional music . . . Nowhere is there a reference to other folksong books or to the popular pocket songsters of the nineteenth century. (210)

Halpert further laments the lack of documentation and the unrepresentative selection of songs. On the positive side, he points out how the selection of tunes reflects the typically heterogeneous character of the fiddler's repertoire.

A review two years later in the *California Folklore Quarterly* (Vol. 2, 1943) by J. Olcutt Sanders pinpoints the same problems, but in a somewhat kindlier tone:

> This thick volume, containing probably the largest collection of United States fiddle tunes in print, will delight the amateur fiddler, but it is not for the critical student. Apparently Ford has more information than he realizes the importance of, and an experienced folklorist might do a great service by working with him to get it in writing. (157)

It is a pity that no academician followed through on Sanders' suggestion. To my knowledge, the only folklorist who ever wrote to Ford in connection with this book (or anything else) was Vance Randolph. In the 1947 *Journal of American Folklore* (Vol. 60, 115-125), Randolph and Frances Emberson presented a survey of "The Collection of Folk Music in the Ozarks." They explained their outline in these terms:

> A good deal of time and energy has been expended by folk song hunters in the Ozark Mountains—the highlands of southern Missouri, northern Arkansas, and eastern Oklahoma. But no attempt has been made, up till now, to write out a chronological account of their activities. In this paper we undertake the task.

[ii]

It seems a good idea to do the job at once, while most of the collectors who have worked in this region are still alive and known to us personally. (115)

After nine pages of detailed accounts, we encounter the following paragraph:

Mr. Ira W. Ford lived near Branson, Missouri, for several years, and it seems likely that some of the songs and fiddle tunes in his *Traditional Music of America* (New York, 1940) were collected in the Ozarks. But the book is innocent of documentation, and the editor doesn't tell the reader where he got his material, except in a very general way. In answer to our letter about this, Mr. Ford writes (May 1, 1946) that "the following tunes included in my work, *Traditional Music of America*, are indigenous to the Missouri Ozark region: 'Great Big Taters in Sandy Land' (p. 39), 'Billy in the Low Ground' (p. 65), 'The Belled Buzzard' (p. 60), 'Bill Simmons' (p. 115), 'Old Hen Cluck' (p. 92), 'Coonie in the Creek' (p. 95), 'Echoes from the Ozarks' (p. 123), 'Ginger Blue' (p. 34), 'Old Yaller Hound' (p. 61), 'Redman's Reel' (p. 116), and 'String Town' (p. 98)." (124)

Evidently Ford was one of the very few collectors working in the Ozarks who was not known personally to either author; he became known to them impersonally only after the fact. That he was not known at all to folklorists beyond that area, save by name, is thus not too surprising.

Ira Ford appeared on the national scene once, in 1940, with the publication of his TRADITIONAL MUSIC OF AMERICA. Before and after that date he went on his way quietly, and at this writing many of the details of his life are still unknown to me. The brief biographical sketch offered below is meant as a first introduction to the author of this book.

Ira William Ford was born on a farm in Grundy County, Missouri, on March 7, 1878, one of the older children in a family of eleven. His father had come there from Kentucky, his mother from Tennessee. His family history, proudly outlined in the foreword, reflects a common pioneer pattern of movement: westward through the southern mountains, with forty-niner treks, often round-trip, to California. Of his youth he wrote to E. P. Dutton:

When quite small, my grandfather and father obtained a large tract of cattle land in South Missouri and moved their families there from the northern part of the state. My education began at a country school near Nevada, Missouri. Selling the cattle ranch, they moved back to North Missouri, buying farm land in Macon County. I finished grade school, also two years high school at La Porte (now called Ten Mile), Missouri.

During those years entertainment was home-made. The elder Ford was an old-time fiddler, and young Ira, who developed a special fascination for that instrument, caught up fiddling techniques and soon joined his father playing for local dances. The tunes which he learned at this time, both from his father and other community fiddlers, were to form the core of the repertoire presented in TRADITIONAL MUSIC OF AMERICA.

After twelve relatively settled years as a printer for various Missouri newspapers, Ford returned to the rugged outdoor life which he preferred:

(I) next spent several years with the Williams Creek Mining & Prospecting Company on lead and zinc, in Missouri. This was followed by four years developing a group of gold claims owned by the Red Rock Mining Company and located in Rio Arriba County, New Mexico. I left there in 1912 and made an extensive prospecting trip in Canada, following the Saskatchewan River from Elk Point, Alberta, far into the Canadian Rockies.

Ford spent his free time hunting, fishing, riding out on horseback. A photograph sent to E. P. Dutton shows him with his two dogs on a wolf hunt at the head of Brazos canyon during his New Mexico mining venture, lean and weathered, a gun and cartridge belt around his hips:

The object of such intense scrutiny by my two dogs, Jack and Snooks, was a monster porcupine who temporarily barred progress of the hunt. They had had previous experience with his kind, much to their annoyance and also to mine, as I had to remove the quills after the combat. However, they were always ready for battle, let it be porky, mountain lion, wolf, coyote, bear or what have you.

Ford's love of "nature in the raw," as he phrased it, led him to become manager of the Bee Creek Tourist Camp, near Lake Taneycomo, in the Missouri Ozarks. I suspect that here, for the first time, confronted by tourist invasions, and of necessity acting a Chamber of Commerce part and developing a sense for what local commodities (whether natural or man-made) might be turned to profit, Ira Ford came to the notion that old-time fiddle tunes could be written down, printed up, and distributed.

When he moved to California in 1930, unable to sustain the resort during depression trials, he already had a "large and varied assortment of notes."

In 1931 the first of four small paper-bound books appeared entitled *Ford's Old Time Fiddle Music*, privately published ("Ford's Publications") in Los Angeles. They sold for one dollar each. Book 1 is subtitled on the front cover "A Collection of 101 Old Tunes that are always NEW"; the title page reads "Ford's Collection of Old Time Fiddle Music, written as played by Fiddlers of Old Time Music in Various parts of America. Compiled and Edited by Ira W. Ford, Hollywood." The foreword calls upon the reader to recognize the role of music in life, and presents the germ of the "Puncheon Floor" tradition later expanded in TRADITIONAL MUSIC IN AMERICA (186-187).

Book 4 came out in 1933, with the following slight but significant changes in legend: "A Collection of Rare Old Tunes that are Always NEW"—"Ford's Collection of Old Time Fiddle Music: Waltzes, Mazourkas, Varsoviennes, Schottisches, Polkas, and Gallops, written as played by The Pioneer Fiddlers of America. Collected, Written, and Arranged by Ira W. Ford." Indeed, four tunes indicate Ford as author: "The Last Waltz," "Smoky Mountain Schottische," "High Point Polka," and "Old Warsaw Polka." He was by hobby a songwriter, although apparently none of his compositions were ever published as such. The Library of Congress Copyright Office lists his name in connection with two song titles: "Don't Go Cheatin' in the Game of Love" (1934), for which he supplied the music (the words, with their hillbillyish title, were written by Olive Surace), and "Love Makes the World Just Right" (1938), for which he served as arranger (words and music by Elsie Cominos).

Not until after Ford had worked on these small publications of fiddle tunes did he conceive the idea of expanding them into TRADITIONAL MUSIC OF AMERICA. This makes the problem of source and that of faithfulness of transcription even more acute, since we do not know precisely which tunes he had brought with him to California and which pieces he wrote out from memory or obtained through correspondence or other means once he was settled on the West Coast. Probably most of the fiddle tunes, particularly those which appeared in the various *Ford's Old Time Fiddle Tunes* in the early 1930's, were those he knew personally, many from his youth, others from his travels and from his Ozark interlude. Almost all of the tunes in Book 1 of *Ford's Old Time Fiddle Tunes* are reproduced in TRADITIONAL MUSIC OF AMERICA, in the earlier

[v]

pages of that volume. In his letter to Randolph and Emberson, Ford specifically credited four of these pieces to the Missouri Ozarks: "Great Big Taters in Sandy Land" (39), "Old Yaller Hound" (61), "Cackling Hen," referred to in the letter as "Old Hen Cluck" (92), and "String Town" (98). Items not carried over from Book 1 include "Come, O Come with Me," "Hours There Were," "Coming Thro' the Rye," "Old Dog Tray," "My Bonnie," "Nellie Bly," "Oh Susanna," "Uncle Ned," "Gentle Annie," "Nellie Was a Lady," "Grave of Uncle True," "Flow Gently Sweet Afton," and "Erin is My Home." All of the tunes in Book 4 reappear, clustered in pages 132-175; between 1933 and 1940 Ford added to these categories only two waltzes, "Poodle Dog Waltz" (139) and "Five Step Waltz" (146); one schottische, "Woodland Schottische" (162); and one polka, "The Esmeralda" (168). We note also that the four tunes credited before to Ira Ford no longer carry his name (136, 158, 169). (I have not seen Books 2 and 3; presumably their contents appear in *Traditional Music of America* in the sections of square dance music, clogs, hornpipes, jigs, reels, and tunes with the violin discorded.)

The fiddle tune traditions, the dance and play-party accounts, the songs and parodies, that is, the material in the second half of TRADITIONAL MUSIC OF AMERICA, all seem to have been put in order later than the first part of the collection—hence, for instance, the physical separation of the fiddle tunes and some of the verses associated with them. Judging from the evidence of analogues, we can accept much of it as traditional. However, we still cannot be sure of sources. Ford undoubtedly knew a good portion of it first-hand, which he wrote out either at the time or later from memory. Once in Los Angeles, he began an extensive correspondence with family and friends in Missouri and elsewhere to secure, verify, and round out information on songs and tunes. And when other devotees of old-time music learned of his project, they sent their contributions to him. The people named in the foreword (9-11), with addresses mostly in Missouri and California, are not necessarily those who provided Ford with tunes or data, although coincidentally the heart of the collection derives from Missouri (and, we might speculate, from the Missouri and Ozark colonies in southern California). Ford wrote explicitly:

> The names given below are of those who have aided me in making possible the publication of this book and who are associated in the many pleasant recollections of old-time dances, play parties and gatherings. I regret that it is impractical to

give a complete listing of those who have rendered such valuable and kindly help, but my sincere gratitude is extended to all. (9)

TRADITIONAL MUSIC OF AMERICA appeared in 1940. The book received short notices in library journals, laudatory and light-hearted comments from newspaper and magazine book reviewers, severe reviews from the folklorists.[1] It was not printed in quantity, and never went into a second printing. Of late it has become frustratingly hard to find, rarely appearing on the used-book market, mysteriously disappearing from libraries. The collection was both invaluable and troublesome, for what it contained and what it did not contain. No one seemed to know quite how to handle it, and so little was done. Ira Ford remained for all practical purposes in a world apart from academic students of traditional American music. After the publication of his book, he continued to work as a machinist in Los Angeles. He left his last job, tool-crib clerk for Hillman-Kelley, in 1944 because of ill health; he died in Pasadena on October 11, 1960.

Ira Ford is remembered by his family and work comrades as a very kind man, courteous, quiet, conservative. He was largely self-educated, and spent spare moments reading and studying. His devotion to his chosen project is reflected both by the time given to it and by the size of the collection. His adeptness as an amateur collector is indicated by his perceptive comments on breaking through rural reserve:

> The writer found most of this music in the rural districts of the different states, among the true descendants of post-Colonial pioneers, tracing its tradition from one community to another until it took final shape from the tangled mass of recollections. But they were difficult to trace. If the inquirer does not "belong" in these regions, he courts failure unless he can adapt himself to the local mode of living and gain the people's confidence. There has always been a feeling of social enmity between the countryfolk and the townspeople. In what is known

[1] The following reviews of Ford's TRADITIONAL MUSIC OF AMERICA have come to my attention: *Booklist*, Vol. 37 (February 15, 1941), 266 (from the *Wisconsin Library Bulletin*, cited below); Frances Alter Boyle, *Library Journal*, Vol. 65 (November 15, 1940), 981; Herbert Halpert, *Journal of American Folklore*, Vol. 54 (1941), 210-211, Douglas Moore, *New York Herald Tribune Books* (September 7, 1941), 13; Abbe Niles, *New Republic*, Vol. 105 (August 4, 1941), 164-165; J. Olcutt Sanders, *California Folklore Quarterly*, Vol. 2 (1943), 157-158; Howard Taubman, *New York Times Book Review* (October 26, 1941), 40; *Wisconsin Library Bulletin*, Vol. 37 (February, 1941), 31.

as the hillbilly districts this feeling is still prevalent, and any stranger sojourning in their midst is looked upon and treated as a "furriner." (8)

Ford obviously took great pride in participating in what he saw as pioneer culture. During his active adult years he sought out raw and rugged terrain, whether western mountains or Ozark uplands, and fell in with the old-timers. He certainly accepted as a compliment Howard Taubman's ambiguous summation of TRADITIONAL MUSIC OF AMERICA in a *New York Times* review: "His product is pure Americana."

Ford's TRADITIONAL MUSIC OF AMERICA, one of our largest collections of fiddle tunes, testifies to the vigor and tenacity of the fiddling tradition in this country. Its reprinting is justified on that ground alone, for our instrumental music has been notoriously neglected by folklorists, at least in their printed publications. Samuel Bayard commented twenty years ago in his exemplary *Hill Country Tunes* (Philadelphia, 1944):

> It must be admitted at the outset that we know little about instrumental folk music in the United States, and study of it cannot yet go far because the tunes themselves remain largely uncollected. Interest in the folk dances has revived lately, but we possess as yet no large quantity of musical material gathered from many different parts of the country—nothing comparable with the mass of our recorded traditional song melodies. (xi)

This lament was echoed as recently as last year, by Joan Moser, in her article on "Instrumental Music of the Southern Appalachians: Traditional Fiddle Tunes" (*North Carolina Folklore*, Vol. 12, 1964, 1-8).

The transcriptions we would like to have for comparison with our own are not readily available. For most of the information on the southern tradition for his *Hill Country Tunes*, Bayard relied on just two compilations, TRADITIONAL MUSIC OF AMERICA, and a commercial effort, F. E. Adam's *Old Time Fiddlers' Favorite Barn Dance Tunes* (Saint Louis, 1938). However, we can profitably supplement academic and commercially printed collections of fiddle tunes with recorded examples, and indeed we must, even though such notation is a long and tedious task.

American fiddling, at least the southern tradition, is probably better documented on disc and tape than in print. From the very beginning of the recording industry's attention to southern white country music in the early 1920's, the fiddler was evident: the first hillbilly disc (1923) was Fiddlin' John Carson's "The Little Old Log Cabin in the Lane/The Old Hen Cackled and the Rooster's Going to Crow" (Okeh 4890), and the first string band to record was The Virginia Reelers, formed by Fiddlin' John in 1924. Columbia quickly followed Okeh's lead, and by November, 1924, had printed a booklet entitled *Familiar Tunes on Fiddle, Guitar, Banjo, Harmonica, and Accordion,* listing records by fiddler Gid Tanner and others "whose names are best known where the square dance has not been supplanted by the fox-trot." Still another company to enter the field, Vocalion, picked as one of its first artists "Uncle Am" Stuart, a champion fiddler from Tennessee. Finally—still in 1924—Victor joined the race, and late in that year placed the following notice in *Talking Machine World,* Vol. 20 (November 12, 1924):

> The old-time fiddler has come into his own again with the music loving public and this fact is reflected in the demand for records of the music of the old fiddlers. The Victor Talking Machine Company has taken cognizance of public interest to issue an attractive four-page folder for dealer distribution with a cover design showing the fiddler presiding over the old-time barn dance, and a caption of "Olde Time Fiddlin' Tunes." In the folder are listed four records by Fiddlin' Powers and family, three records by A. C. (Eck) Robertson, and two Southern mountaineer songs on a record by Vernon Dalhart with fiddle accompaniment. (178)[2]

Thousands of such 78 rpm discs were released between 1923 and World War II, when new musical styles began to develop and 45 rpm and long-playing records gradually replaced the 78's. For years they were unattainable, or they circulated within the small and mostly non-academic clan of hillbilly record collectors. Now many of them are again available, having been deposited in the John Edwards Memorial Foundation (UCLA). The Library of Congress has also made field recordings of fiddle tunes, although its collecting project began in earnest some ten years after the recording industry had become active in many of the same areas. The Library of Congress has issued some of these tunes commercially; see, for instance, scattered pieces on AAFS L2, L5, L9, L16, L20, L21, and L55. A number of valuable LP reissues of old 78 rpm discs have appeared, some devoted entirely to fiddle

---

[2] For a detailed account of that period, see Archie Green, "Hillbilly Music: Source and Symbol," *Journal of American Folklore,* Vol. 78 (July, 1965), from which the information above was excerpted.

music. Among the first were *Mountain Frolic* (Brunswick BL 59000) and the Harry Smith anthology *American Folk Music* (Folkways FA 2951-2953). Later came *A Collection of Mountain Fiddle Music* (County 501), *Old-time Southern Dance Music: The String Bands* (Old-Timey X-100), and others. Freshly recorded presentations range from *The 37th Old-Time Fiddlers Convention at Union Grove, North Carolina* (Folkways FA 2434) to *Fiddlin' Arthur Smith and the Dixie Liners* (Starday SLP 202). Indicative of the revival of interest in traditional fiddle music among the younger enthusiasts today are the new release by Tracy Schwarz, *Learn to Fiddle Country Style* (Folkways FI 8359), and the attention to that instrument, with some transcriptions based on discs, in the *New Lost City Ramblers Song Book* (New York, 1964).

Of course, the field recordings of other collectors comprise a rich source of material for study and comparison. The chief problem is that many collectors are not known to each other; we are fortunate and enlightened when such people reach print, for instance, Bayard and Moser (cited earlier), or Marion Unger Thede, who contributed "Traditional Fiddling" to *Ethnomusicology*, Vol. 6 (1962), 19-24, or for that matter, Ira Ford. One solution for collectors who are temporarily unable or unlikely to ever publish what they have gathered is to deposit their recordings in a central and working archive, such as the Library of Congress Archive of Folk Song or the Indiana University Archives of Traditional Music.[3] Once recordings, manuscripts, books, folios, and other types of documentation are available to circulate, study of this aspect of tradition will be potentially much more profitable.

It is curious that in America most traditional instrumental music has been gathered by amateurs and by commercial concerns. D. K. Wilgus suggests in *Anglo-American Folksong Scholarship Since 1898* that the academic collectors neglected music because of incompetence and lack of interest, or because of the social distance between native musician and visiting folklorist (153-154). Yet one of the most productive collectors in the southern mountains, Cecil Sharp, who certainly did not suffer from lack of musicianship, excluded instrumental music from his *English Folk Songs from the Southern Appalachians* (2 vols., London, 1932); all the "jigs" presented were obtained from singing. He notated several fiddle tunes but did not include them in the 1917 first edition

---

[3] Among the larger field collections of fiddle tunes in the Archives of Traditional Music are those of Norman Cazden (Adirondacks), Peter Hoover (general southern tradition), Elli-Kaija Köngäs Maranda (Finnish-American), Lyle Mayfield (Illinois), and myself (Indiana, Illinois, Ozarks).

(Vol. 1, xxvii). Maud Karpeles explained why they were also withheld from the 1932 edition:

> The instrumental tunes which were played as accompaniments to the dance were of little value. A few dance-tunes were noted by Cecil Sharp, but these apart from the method and style of their playing have but little interest, and so I have not reproduced them. (Vol. 1, xviii)

The intense concern with folksong in the United States has been such that we might be tempted to doubt the existence of a viable instrumental tradition. Not only the abundance of early commercial and field recordings mentioned above, but also scattered written reports speak against this negative suggestion. One such account was provided by Louise Rand Bascom, in "Ballads and Songs of Western North Carolina" (*Journal of American Folklore*, Vol. 22, 1909, 238-250). After describing "those interesting celebrations known as Fiddlers' Conventions," she commented on style and spread:

> Strangely enough, no matter how sad the words and music may be, they are always rendered as rapidly as is compatible with the skill of the musician, and without inflection. The tunes are played at all of the dances, whistled and sung by the men and boys everywhere. The mountaineer who cannot draw music from the violin, the banjo, or the "French Harp," is probably non-existent. (238)

Closer to Ira Ford's territory, Vance Randolph has offered four and a half pages of nothing but Ozark fiddle tune titles, from which we may judge the extent of the tradition there.[4] His sad preface to "The Names of Ozark Fiddle Tunes" is worth quoting for the light it sheds on the difficulties of gathering instrumental music, when an interested collector can be found:

> For more than thirty years I was accustomed to disport myself at dances in the Ozark country, and heard many of the tradi-

---

[4] It is axiomatic that lists of tune titles are of limited value. Still, their length and variety are some indication of the strength of local or individual tradition. Interesting catalogs appear, for instance, in the following: Carl Carmer, *Stars Fell on Alabama* (New York, 1934), 275-277; Joan Moser, "Instrumental Music of the Southern Appalachians: Traditional Fiddle Tunes," *North Carolina Folklore*, Vol. 12 (1964), 3-4; Howard Odum, *An American Epoch* (New York, 1930), 201-206 (cited by Bayard, xxiv); Vance Randolph, "The Names of Ozark Fiddle Tunes," *Midwest Folklore*, Vol. 4 (1954), 81-86; J. Olcutt Sanders, "Honor the Fiddler," in *Texian Stomping Grounds*, Texas Folklore Society Publications No. 17 (Austin, 1941), 88-89; Lloyd Shaw, *Cowboy Dances* (revised, Caldwell, Idaho, 1952), 34-35; Marion Unger Thede, "Traditional Fiddling," *Ethnomusicology*, Vol. 6 (1962), 22-23.

tional fiddle-tunes. I wanted to collect these items, but have no musical training and am not competent to write down the tunes. Once, in the early 1940's, I borrowed a portable recorder from Alan Lomax and made about a hundred disc recordings for the Library of Congress. But I never had money enough to buy a recorder of my own. The foundations and learned societies refused to finance a study of backwoods fiddle-tunes, so I reluctantly abandoned the project. (81)

By far the most interesting account of early music in Missouri is that by Francis O'Neill, the Chicago policeman of Irish ancestry, who, like Ira Ford, devoted his life to gathering the old fiddle tunes. O'Neill served for a time as schoolteacher at Edina, in Knox County, Missouri; from that experience he reported the following:

Mr. Broderick, the school director with whom I boarded at Edina, was a native of Galway and a fine performer on the flute. Not a week passed during the winter months without a dance or two being held among the farmers. Such a motley crowd—fiddlers galore, and each with his instrument. Irish, Germans, French—types of their respective races—and the gigantic Kentuckians, whose heads were endangered by the low ceilings, crowded in, and never a misunderstanding or display of ill-nature marred those gatherings. Seated behind the fiddler, intent on picking up the tunes, was my accustomed post, but how much was memorized on those occasions cannot now be definitely stated. Three tunes, however, distinctly obtrude on my memory, viz.: A reel played by Ike Forrester, the "Village Blacksmith," which was named after him; "My Love is Fair and Handsome," Mr. Broderick's favorite reel; and a quickstep, which I named "Nolan, the Soldier." Nolan had been a fifer in the Confederate army during the Civil War. His son was an excellent drummer, and both gave free exhibitions of their skill on the public square at Edina to enliven the evenings while the weather was fine.[5]

It happens that Knox County is not far to the east of Grundy County, where Ira Ford was born, and adjacent on the northeast to Macon County, where Ford grew up; O'Neill's account covers the decade just before Ford's birth. This passage is thus perhaps our best indication of the environment in which Ford developed as a fiddler and formed the

[5] Francis O'Neill, *Irish Folk Music* (Chicago, 1910), 16-17. This energetic collector of Irish musical tradition also deserves study and recognition. His most important collection, *Music of Ireland* (Chicago, 1903), contains 1850 melodies, 1225 of which are dance tunes.

heart of his repertoire. We note the singling out of "the gigantic Kentuckians," and recall that the elder Ford had come from that state. We note the nationalities mentioned—Irish, German, French—and find that of the tunes in Ford which are cited by Bayard (approximately one fifth of Bayard's entries carry such notes), foreign references are predominantly Anglo-Irish and continental.

A few points deserve more extensive study than will be possible here. Ford was not provided with pre-cast notions of what comprised a traditional collection, but was concerned with setting forth the musical lore that seemed important to him. He was alert to the ready movement between vocal and instrumental renditions of a melody (18), and also did not make an artificial separation when it came to the countless snatches of free-floating verse sung now against the fiddle, now alone.[6] A handful of folklorists have commented upon this; Maud Karpeles, for instance, wrote of the Appalachians:

> Of greater interest (than the instrumental tunes) were the Jigs, which were sung often as ditties on their own, but their primary purpose was apparently to serve as an accompaniment to step-dances, or "hoe-downs," as they were called, and for this reason, perhaps, they were frowned upon by certain sections of the community. The words appeared to be chosen from a large stock of phrases and fitted at random to the tunes. (Vol. 1, xviii)

The most organized and spirited discussion of these "fiddle songs" is Robert W. Gordon's article by that title in *Folk-Songs of America* (National Service Bureau Publication No. 73-S, New York, 1938, 71-77); his impression was that the verses served a secondary function:

> The words may add brightness and relieve monotony, but as long as the fiddler continues to furnish the musical rhythm the dance will go on. Hence the stanzas tend to come at irregular intervals, often in groups. One singer—whether onlooker, dancer, or fiddler matters not at all—sings a single verse. That

---

[6] Ford, 27ff. Vance Randolph, *Ozark Mountain Folks* (New York, 1932), 71-72 comments on another aspect of the link of words to melody:

> Obscene but sometimes amusing verses have been set to nearly every one of the old fiddle-tunes, and are known to almost everybody. Familiar with these words myself, I have often been amazed at the distinctness with which the fiddle seems to pronounce them. Some of these wicked old hill-billies can "make a fiddle talk" in very truth, but it is conversation of a sort which cannot be printed here.

suggests another and another until a series or sequence of similar verses is built up. (71-72)

Thus we find that between the first appearance of some of the tunes in his *Old Time Fiddle Tunes* (1931-1933) and their reappearance in TRADITIONAL MUSIC OF AMERICA (1940), Ford appended new stanzas, indicated in parentheses below the tune by "verses on page—" or "other verses on page —."

Other bits of verbal lore which sometimes cling tenaciously to fiddle tunes are the tune legends, Ford's "traditions." These stories may, of course, become attached to more than a single tune, and go through versions of their own. In my own experience, "Uncle Absie" Morrison, an old-time Arkansas fiddler, predictably told the story of certain tunes, mostly from military history, whenever he played them; and he did not tell the stories without picking up his fiddle to present the march, siege, or retreat. In these special cases the genre became something larger than either fiddle tune or legend.

We find passing references in TRADITIONAL MUSIC OF AMERICA to two more aspects of this instrumental complex: the custom of beating the fiddle strings with knitting needles (129-130), and the important institution of the fiddlers' convention (183). It is possible that Ford himself participated in such contests; obviously he was very familiar with them. He gave more attention to the practice of using different tunings for different pieces (125ff.), as has virtually everyone else who has encountered it.[7] The full story of these peripheral phenomena, however, remains to be written.

———————

TRADITIONAL MUSIC OF AMERICA was first published on the eve of our entry into World War II, when frontier life and other Americana offered particularly comforting images of strength, security, and independence. Ira Ford wished to "preserve and revive" those traditions which he felt had grown up with the nation and which he identified with it. Writing more as a member of a folk community than as a folklorist, looking from the inside out, he documented much which might otherwise have been lost, and so fulfilled as best he could the first half of his intent. The second half was of course not in his power to control; the time

———

[7] See, for example, Bayard, xv; Moser, 4, 8; Sanders, 80; Sharp, Vol. 1, xxvii; and Unger, 19. On one of the Library of Congress albums, AAFS L21, *Anglo-American Songs and Ballads*, edited by Duncan Emrich, various fiddle tunings are demonstrated (side A, band 2).

was not right for its realization. It is fitting that his book is being re-printed now, during a spirited revival of interest in old-time music, in the people who shaped it, in the environment in which it flourished. Were Ford with us, he would certainly be pleased.*

JUDITH McCULLOH

Archives of Traditional Music
Indiana University
May, 1965

* My thanks for material assistance and encouragement go especially to the following persons: Ed Cray (Los Angeles); Mrs. F. T. McElroy (Phoenix, Arizona) and Mrs. Richard Oeltjen (Los Angeles), younger sisters of Ira Ford; Elliott Graham, of E. P. Dutton (New York); Archie Green, of the University of Illinois (Urbana); and Mrs. Alicia James, of the John Edwards Memorial Foundation (UCLA).

TRADITIONAL MUSIC OF AMERICA

TRADITIONAL
MUSIC
OF
AMERICA

Ira W. Ford

NEW YORK

E. P. Dutton and Company, Inc.

1940

TABLE OF CONTENTS

FOREWORD

AFTER many years of research, the author has endeavored to record in this book, with other material bearing on the subject, that which is recognized as the traditional music of America.

The wide range of country visited while assembling this collection makes it musically representative of pioneer settlements ranging from the Atlantic to the Pacific and from Mexico to the Canadian border. A very large percentage of it was collected from pioneers who were still here and has never before been written or printed, having been handed down from ear to ear by people of bygone generations. The fiddle tunes were written as the writer heard them played by community fiddlers and, in some instances, he learned them from the actual composers. The tunes, as played by different fiddlers, vary, and some of them may be found under several names. However, in tracing this music, only the most universally accepted versions of the tunes and their titles have been included. Unfortunately, many of the old tunes and songs of early pioneer days have long since been forgotten and most of the traditions are but a fading memory among the few. But the most popular of the old fiddle tunes have endured throughout the development of every state and territory in the Union and still remain favorite dance tunes of today, despite the new additions.

This music had its inception in post-Colonial days. The famous scouts, Daniel Boone, David Crockett, Kit Carson and others, blazed the trails of exploration into new territory. Civilization, of the days of ox-teams and covered wagons, log houses, powder horns and bullet moulds began its slow steady march of conquest across a new continent. As increasing population demanded it, frontiers were steadily pushed forward and pioneer settlements were established in many widely separated locations. The trails were beset with all the dangers of the wilds and travel was unsafe, save in numbers of sufficient strength for the protection of all. Therefore there was very little association between the folks of neighboring settlements, until the spread of civilization tamed the country and it became more densely populated.

Within the social life of these isolated communities the growth of folk-song and traditions was a natural sequence. So, handed down to us through the years are the old fiddle tunes with their traditions; the quaint calls of the American square dance; the old-time play party songs; children's play songs and games of the old-time village green, and other songs of entertainment. All these depict the characteristics and activities of our American ancestry more vividly than written history has ever done.

The aim of this work is to preserve this folk-music and the traditions of those courageous souls who conquered the wilderness, the deserts and the plains and gave to the world a new nation.

America, being one of the youngest among nations, gives the modern research worker the advantage of having to delve but a short distance, so that, from its comparatively recent past, most of the folklore in song, music and tradition may be preserved. And the rural districts of this country are rich in tradition. The writer found most of this music in the rural districts of the different states, among the true descendants of post-Colonial pioneers, tracing its tradition from one community to another until it took final shape from the tangled mass of recollections. But they were difficult to trace. If the inquirer does not "belong" in these regions, he courts failure unless he can adapt himself to the local mode of living and gain the people's confidence. There has always been a feeling of social enmity between the countryfolk and the townspeople. In what is known as the hill-billy districts this feeling is still prevalent, and any stranger sojourning in their midst is looked upon and treated as a "furriner."

The violin was about the only musical instrument possessed by the first generation of pioneers, the dulcimer, melodeon and reed organ coming later. The fiddle, light of weight and easy to transport, was present at all their social gatherings. A good fiddle was the chief pride of its owner. There are many old fiddles still in use, made more than a hundred years ago by clever woodworkers equally skilled in converting the forest trees into homes. From the old fiddle tunes, composed and played by these pioneers on their home-made fiddles, sprang many of the later songs that accompanied the progress of the nation. Thus, the old fiddle tunes became the foundation of the traditional music of America.

The writer is a descendant of American pioneers. My great-great-grandparents White came from Virginia and Kentucky. A great-great-grandmother Ferguson, born shortly after the Revolutionary War, was a sister of Frank Thomas, a governor of Maryland. Her child Catherine, my great-grandmother Parcels, was born in Elizabethtown, Kentucky, in 1796. My great-grandparents Cochrane and great-grandparents Hubbard, Rawling B., born 1806, and wife Phebe, came from Virginia and Kentucky. My great-grandfather Elias Ford and wife White settled in Virginia. James H. Ford, born 1812, my paternal grandfather, and grandmother, Permelia Cochrane, born 1815, were natives of Kentucky and pioneer settlers in Grundy County, Missouri. My grandfather was also a California pioneer of the 49's. My maternal grandparents, Thomas B. Parcels, born 1817, and Rebecca J. Hubbard, born 1830, were from Kentucky. My father, Thomas B. Ford, and mother, Sarah Elizabeth Parcels, were also Southerners. Some of this post-Colonial music was thus acquired from my immediate family, as well as from other sources.

The names given below are of those who have aided me in making possible the publication of this book and who are associated in the many pleasant recollections of old-time dances, play parties and gatherings. I regret that it is impractical to give a complete listing of those who have rendered such valuable and kindly help, but my sincere gratitude is extended to all. Many of them have now passed the Great Divide, while others are scattered.

Among the old-timers were:

James H. Ford. Thomas Hays, Virginia, settler in Grundy County, Missouri. Thomas Parcels, Kentucky, settler in Adair County, Missouri. Mate Gibson, South Carolina, settler in Sullivan County, Missouri. William McCracken, Ohio, settler in Sullivan

County, Missouri. Tate Gupton, Indiana, settler in Grundy County, Missouri. Charles Tracy, New Hampshire, settler in Macon County, Missouri. Samuel Lane, Tennessee, settler in Macon County, Missouri. Withrow Morris, Virginia, settler in Vernon County, Missouri. James Blackwell, North Carolina, settler in Vernon County, Missouri. Many of these people were in the gold rush to California in 1849.

Coming down to our own day I may mention:

Mr. and Mrs. George Davis, Los Angeles, California. Mrs. Ida Roberts, Los Angeles, California. Mr. and Mrs. F. T. McElroy, Phoenix, Arizona. Mr. and Mrs. Howard Montgomery, Boise City, Oklahoma. Mrs. Nettie Parcels, Riverside, California. Mr. and Mrs. Glenn A. Hall, Castella, California. Mr. A. D. McKenzie, Portland, Oregon. Mr. and Mrs. J. E. Hillenbrand, Los Angeles, California. Mrs. Elizabeth Rubly, Los Angeles, California. Mrs. Anna Mockenhaupt, Los Angeles, California. Mr. C. A. Caton, Los Angeles, California. Mr. James Merrill, Los Angeles, California. Mr. D. D. Chapman, Los Angeles, California. Mr. Charles S. Matson, Los Angeles, California. Mr. and Mrs. Oscar Smothers, Los Angeles, California. Mr. J. Vandiver, Los Tusas, New Mexico. Mr. Ben McClaren, Wiley, Colorado. Mr. James Gill, Denver, Colorado. Mr. John Bradshaw, Wellington, Kansas. Mr. Frederic Bell, Kansas City, Kansas. Mr. J. W. Davis, Riverton, Nebraska. Mr. George E. Davis, Kansas City, Missouri. Mr. and Mrs. R. B. Goodrich, Kansas City, Missouri. Mr. George Redman, Atlanta, Missouri. Mr. Frank Parcels, Kirksville, Missouri. Miss Isadore Clament, Sedalia, Missouri. Mr. Rufus Brazil, Branson, Missouri. Mr. M. Fream, Harrison, Arkansas. Mr. and Mrs. Sidney Johnston, Austin, Texas. Mr. John Marshall, Shreveport, Louisiana. Mr. George Stancil, Atlanta, Georgia. Mr. George Galligan, Herrin, Illinois. Mr. Pete Slicter, St. Louis, Missouri. Mr. John B. Ford, Orlando, Florida. Mr. and Mrs. Dick Oeltjen, Los Angeles, California. Mr. and Mrs. Archie O. Ford, Los Angeles, California. Mrs. Elsie Cominos, Alhambra, California. Mr. Herbert F. Key, Alhambra, California. Mr. Benjamin F. Ford, Kansas City, Missouri. Mr. Edward Neudeck, Branson, Missouri. Mr. and Mrs. John B. Ford, Versailles, Missouri. Mr. Harold Hall, Los Angeles, California. Mr. James T. Ford, Buffalo, Missouri. Mr. Con Donohue, Sedalia, Missouri. Mr. and Mrs. Hardy M. Deavenport, Memphis, Tennessee.

It would require another volume to give the names of friends and acquaintances, not to mention the story of the occasions — play parties, dances and other gatherings — attended by the writer, during a research which covered most of his lifetime.

There is much undiscovered material still existent, which will no doubt be recorded in time as the history of American music is compiled. Until such time the writer, as a descendant of American pioneers, offers this contribution.

IRA W. FORD

Los Angeles, California
1940

Special mention must be made of Miss J. T. C. Brander, whose expert and untiring help on the manuscript of this book was highly appreciated by the author.

CHARACTERIZATION

CHARACTERIZATION

THIS BOOK gives a picture of America's early social and work activities, expressed in some of its unwritten traditional music and history.

The traditions and stories of this music have been collected in various parts of the country, in many instances in the immediate locality in which they had their origin.

The old-time play party songs, the children's play songs of the old-time village green and the lively old dance tunes of fiddle lore are all representative of the robust social and work activities in American country life during the different stages of development of the United States. Gatherings such as the singing school, debating society, spelling bee, berry picking, school exhibition, and sports and pastimes including the shooting match, fox hunt, coon hunt, fishing party, were all used as occasion for parties wherein originated many of these tunes and songs. So, too, the work gatherings. Here the fraternalism of the early pioneers was portrayed as they helped one another clear new lands and construct their homes, trade work in harvesting and many other ways. Rail splitting, clapboard riving, wood chopping, log rolling, house or barn raising, threshing, corn husking bee, all had their turn. (At "corn shuckin'" woe betide the girl who happened to remove the shuck from a red ear of corn — she was sure to be kissed by some lucky swain who could match that red ear. Many a timid girl at her first husking bee has removed the husk from each ear of corn with a comical expression of dreaded anticipation).

TRADITIONAL FIDDLE TUNES

A great many of the song sketches connected with the old traditional fiddle tunes have as their subject the opossum, coon and dog. Today these animals are associated with the sport of hunting. But to the pioneer, the skins and furs were of great economic importance, as their trade value represented about the only means he had of obtaining the "store boughten" things he needed. The coonskin was always in demand, as nearly everyone wore a coonskin cap. It was not unusual for a man to "swop" a cow or "hoss" for a coon dog, and maybe give a gallon of good "co'n licker" to boot. At that time an average grade coonskin was worth half a dollar. The skins of the opossum, weasel and other commoner animals ranged in value down to a few cents, while that of the fox, mink and otter represented the higher denominations of this trade money. In the course of transactions a customer often received some of the cheaper skins in making change. Especially was this so where there was more than one store at the "tradin' post." And at the trading post and the mill where the settlers carried their grist to be ground into meal, there were always fiddles available. It was during their occasional meetings that the fiddlers "larned" these tunes from each other and passed them on from ear to ear. From ear to ear they have followed the frontiers as they pushed forward, down to the present time.

TRADITIONAL DANCE CALLS

The origin of many old-time dance calls may be traced to certain periods in the nation's history. They also picture the pioneer's early dangers, work activities and pleasures. For instance:

Squaw in the cane-brake,
Papoose on her back,
When you meet your partner,
Take a back track!

The above would suggest that it had its origin in the early days of the South, when the Indians were a hazard to the settlers. A later example is:

Cradle that wheat and cradle that rye,
Buckwheat batter and huckleberry pie.
Gingerbread pudding and brandy mincemeat,
Promenade around till you find a seat!

This also recalls the time when harvesting machinery was unknown, when the cradle and the sickle, the hand-rake and the flail were the only implements they had for harvesting grain.

The American square dance figures have always varied according to the style of calling evolved in each community. From earliest times up to the present, trick calls have been invented by callers to add spice and fun to the dance. And, like songs and musical numbers, some of them survived, while others had a short-lived popularity.

THE OLD-TIME PLAY PARTY

The old-time American play party is a sort of compromise that was conceded to young folks whose parents and well-meaning friends did not approve of the old-time dance.

All along the way of human progress there have been people in every generation who looked upon the amusements and frivolities of youth with disfavor. Thus, the dance was thought by many good church people, and was preached from the pulpit, as the open door to perdition. The melodies of its old tunes were likened to the wailing of lost souls from the shores of desolation and were believed to have been brought out in some mystic way through the violin's tones by Old Scratch himself! Indeed, a fiddler was considered by these good folks to be a sort of Pied Piper leading his flock towards the untold horrors of "Fiddlers' Green," a place beyond Hades, both in direction and in severity of punishment.

However, the exuberant spirit of youth will be served. So there came into being the play party, a modified form of the old-time dance, the main difference being that lively songs were invented to take the place of the fiddler and his tunes.

CHILDREN'S PLAY-SONGS OF THE VILLAGE GREEN

Children's games and play songs of long ago were patterned somewhat after the play party of their elders.

The place selected by the little folks for their outdoor games

17

was sometimes called by them "the village green." Here, while at play on a grassy carpet of green, they invented many of the simple and interesting games and songs that have lived on down the years.

Songs of pioneer days, and up to the Civil War, are closely interwoven with old traditional fiddle tunes. There may be found bars from one or more of the old tunes mixed through many of the songs, while in some instances the words are set to the fiddle tune note for note.

In another manner, fiddlers who played by ear learned the song melodies of the day and arranged their own interpretation. These were afterward handed down as fiddle tunes under the titles of the original songs. Some of these tunes, being in two-four and six-eight time, were used to dance by, while others were played only for musical entertainment.

The southern Negro banjo interpretations also played an important part in the moulding of many of the traditional tunes. The darkies sang, whether at work or at play, and along with the "Spirituals" they originated many other songs of entertainment in a lighter mode.

The following sketch is an example of the spontaneity of Negro song:

> *Dinah.* "Petah, you come in to dinnah."
> *Peter.* "Kain' you wait till Ah hoes dis row?"
> *Dinah.* "Come along heah, you wicked sinnah."
> *Peter.* "Kain' you wait till Ah hoes dis row?"
>
> *Duet.* Keep dat 'possum wa'm.
> Keep dat 'possum wa'm.
> Keep dat 'possum wa'm.
> An' wait till Ah hoes dis row.

Thus, we have a characterization of social and work activities covering some of the unwritten traditional music and history of America.

18

ACCOMPANIMENTS

ACCOMPANIMENTS

This simple system of accompaniment originated on the melodeon and the reed organ. The chords and patterns are arranged below as they have been played since pioneer days, and handed down with the old American fiddle tunes. When played on the piano, with accented bass, they form the very best background for these old-time melodies. Extra notes should never be cued in, as they obscure the rhythm.

There is a dissonance in this style of accompaniment, which changes in the progressive notes of the bass. The old-timers, knowing nothing of the rules of harmony, called this dissonance the "discord change" when they "seconded to" or "chorded to" these traditional square dance tunes in two-four and six-eight time.

With regard to the waltzes, schottisches, and so on, these would require individual arrangements, for the most part. However, it is not possible to do so in this necessarily limited work.

By changing the tempo, these chord arrangements serve for accompaniments to fiddle tunes in six-eight time.

MAJOR

C / CHORD

MAJOR

D / CHORD

MAJOR

E / CHORD

MAJOR

F / CHORD

23

MAJOR
G / CHORD

MAJOR
A / CHORD

TRADITIONAL MUSIC OF THE
AMERICAN FIDDLER

TRADITIONAL MUSIC

of

THE AMERICAN FIDDLER

AMERICAN square dance tunes, as played by fiddlers who have learned them by ear, have a distinctive type of rhythm. They differ from the jigs, reels and hornpipes of other countries. Most of the American tunes have a definite ending and repeat. The same class of dance tunes in other countries, especially Scotland and Ireland, play round and round ad libitum, or to the end of the dance. Scottish and Irish tunes, come down through several generations of American fiddlers, have been changed to the style of rhythm peculiar to those of American origin.

The song verses attached to old American fiddle tunes are the result of spontaneous outbursts of callers at old-time dances. These verses, in most cases, are meaningless and have no bearing on any part, or to the call of the dance. They are merely stopgaps used by callers to fill in between the necessary promptings in the figures of the set. These nonsense rhymes have been handed down with the old fiddle tunes and, with variations, may still be heard at old-time dances at the present time.

THE WAGONEER

(Tradition on page 181)

It is more difficult to play the above original tune, the "Wagoneer," than the modern one entitled "Wagner." So, through long usage, the tune has been simplified as below, preserving the easy swing and rhythm peculiar to these old American dance tunes.

WAGNER

FLANNEL JACKET

'POSSUM UP A GUM STUMP

Possum up a gum stump, coonie in the holler,

 Little gal at our house, fat as she can waller.

Saddle up the old nag, martingale and collar.

 Fetch her down to my house, I'll give you half a dollar.

SMOKY MOUNTAIN

OLD MOLLY HARE

Old Molly Hare,

What you doin' there,

Diggin' out a post hole

And scratchin' out yore hair?

(Tradition on page 193)

MASON'S HORNPIPE

CORINTHIAN HORNPIPE

McLEOD'S REEL

MISSISSIPPI SAWYER

(Tradition on page 183)

ALL AROUND THE TOWN

PADDY WHACK

A LIFE ON THE OCEAN WAVE

(Verses on page 408)

LITTLE BROWN JUG

(Verses on page 415)

BOBTAIL HOSS

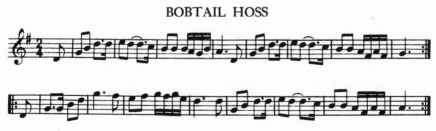

JOHNSON GAL

D.S. al Fine

GINGER BLUE

D.C. al Fine

34

SAIL AWAY, LADY

WILD HORSE

GRANNY WILL YOUR DOG BITE?

Granny, will your dog bite, cow kick, cat scratch?

Granny, will your hen peck, sow root the corn patch?

Granny, will your duck quack, old grey goose hatch?

Granny, will your dog bite? "Yes, child, No!"

BETTY BAKER

I went down for to see Betty Baker,

She was asleep and the Devil couldn't wake 'er.

She wouldn't stir and her mother wouldn't shake 'er,

Long time ago.

PEWTER MUG

RUN, NIGGER, RUN

Run, nigger, run, or the patterollers'll get you.

Run, nigger, run, for you'd better get away.

(See play-party song "Jim-Along Josey" on page 239)

OLD SOLDIER

There was an old soldier and he had a wooden leg,

He had no tobacco and tobacco he would beg.

Says this old soldier: "Won't you give me a chew?"

Says t'other old soldier: "I'll be darned if I do."

(See verses "There Was a Little Hen" on page 440)

CLIMBING UP THE GOLDEN STAIR

(See song on page 283)

FISHER'S HORNPIPE

GREAT BIG TATERS IN SANDY LAND

Great big taters in sandy land.

We-all dig 'em out as fast as we can.

The folks all buy 'em from a foolish man,

Raisin' great big taters in sandy land.

(Other verses on page 180)

(Tradition on page 179)

HOE CAKE

ANDY McSHANE

POP GOES THE WEASEL

(Verses on page 411)

(Parody "Pop Goes the Question" on page 444)

PADDY, WON'T YOU DRINK SOME GOOD OLD CIDER?

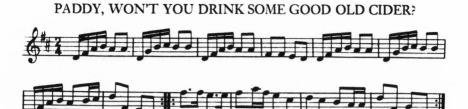

Paddy, won't you drink some,
Paddy, won't you drink some,
Paddy, won't you drink some
Good old cider?

RIPPYTOE RAY

And a damn good fiddler was he.
But all the tune that he could play
Was Rippytoe Ray, oh, Rippytoe Ray,
Oh, Rippytoe Ray, oh, ree-e-e.
Oh, Rippytoe Ray.

(Tune with violin "discorded," on page 127)

CHICKEN REEL

MINNIE MOORE

SHAWL DANCE

D.C. al Fine

THE WIND THAT SHAKES THE BARLEY

GILDEROY

IRISH WASHWOMAN

IRONTOWN

RAG TIME ANNIE

THE CUCKOO

The Cuckoo's a pretty bird, she sings as she flies.
She brings us glad tidings and tells us no lies.

AULD LANG SYNE

(Parody verses "The Mule" on page 434)

FORKED DEER

(Tradition on page 184)

LISTEN TO THE MOCKING BIRD

OLD PORK BOSOM

ARKANSAS TRAVELER

(Tradition on page 188)

BLUE MOUNTAIN BOYS REEL

SAILOR'S HORNPIPE

RYE STRAW

UNCLE JOE

Don't you want to go to heaven, Uncle Joe! Uncle Joe!

Don't you want to go to heaven, by and by?

Don't you want to go to heaven, Uncle Joe! Uncle Joe!

Where the 'possum and the sweet potatoes grow up in the sky?

PICNIC ROMP

LEATHER BRITCHES

OLD AUNT JENNY

Who's been here since I've been gone?
Who's been here since I've been gone?
Who's been here since I've been gone?
Old Aunt Jenny with her nightcap on.

OLD GREY GOOSE

ACROSS THE RIVER

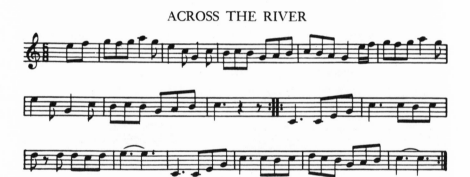

SOLDIER'S JOY

49

RICKETTS HORNPIPE

REUBEN

Reuben, Reuben, I've been thinkin',
'Bout this matrimonial sea.
If the ship should start to sinkin'
What in the world becomes of me?

OLD TAYLOR

TWINKLE LITTLE STAR

(Verses on page 401)

OLD GREGORY

51

RUSTIC DANCE

TEN MILE

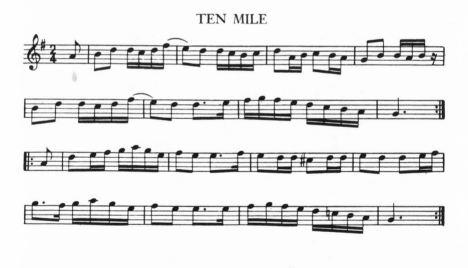

MONEY MUSK

(Dance Call on page 214)

52

HASTE TO THE WEDDING
(Perry's Victory)

DURANG'S HORNPIPE

BUFFALO GIRLS

(Verses on page 409)

SPLITTIN' RAILS

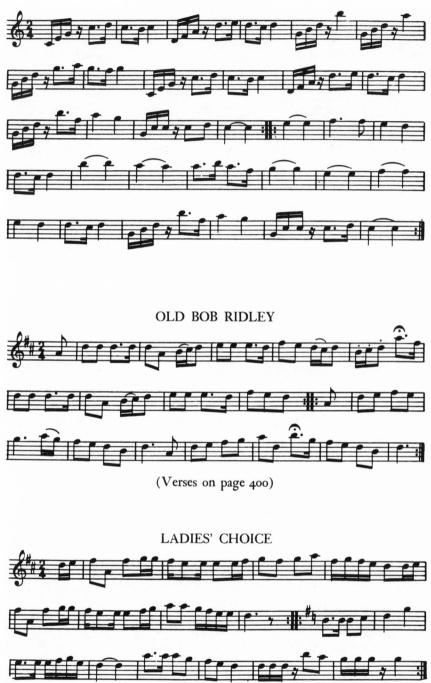

OLD BOB RIDLEY

(Verses on page 400)

LADIES' CHOICE

SPRIG OF SHILLELAGH

YOUNG DAN TUCKER

(Tradition on page 182)

OLD DAN TUCKER

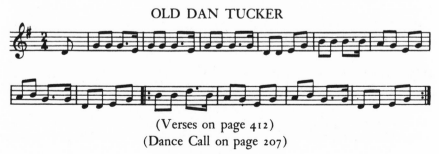

(Verses on page 412)
(Dance Call on page 207)

NATCHEZ UNDER THE HILL

ROSIN THE BOW

Oh, I'd like to be buried, I'm thinking,
   To the tune of Old Rosin the Bow.
Go dig a deep hole in the meadow,
   And in it toss Rosin the Bow.

Chorus

And in it toss Rosin the Bow,
   And in it toss Rosin the Bow.
Go dig a deep hole in the meadow
   And in it toss Rosin the Bow.

Get five or six jovial young fellows,
   And stand them all round in a row.

Let them drink out of half-gallon bottles

To the name of Old Rosin the Bow.

Chorus

To the name of Old Rosin the Bow,

To the name of Old Rosin the Bow.

Let them drink out of half-gallon bottles

To the name of Old Rosin the Bow.

(Parody verses, "Paddy's Curiosity Shop," on page 432)
(Song, "Old Rosin the Beau," on page 392)
(Tune with violin "discorded," on page 127)

PUNCHEON FLOOR

(Tradition on page 186)

LONESOME KATY

STEP TO THE MUSIC, JOHNNY

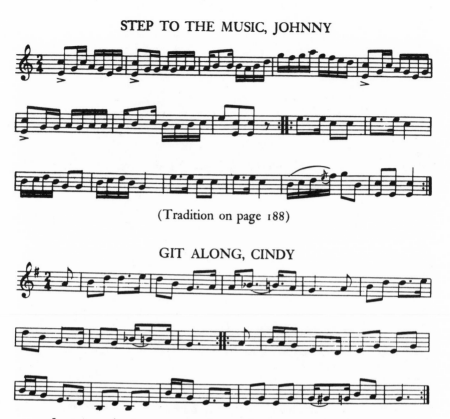

(Tradition on page 188)

GIT ALONG, CINDY

I went out in the new ground to gather a sack of corn,

The 'possum set the dogs on me and the raccoon blowed the horn.

Oh, git along home, Cindy, Cindy, git along home, Cindy, Cindy.

Git along home, Cindy, Cindy, it'll soon be sundown.

TIP TOE, PRETTY BETTY MARTIN

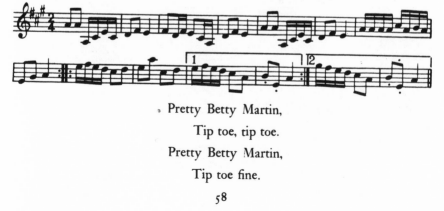

Pretty Betty Martin,

Tip toe, tip toe.

Pretty Betty Martin,

Tip toe fine.

LUCY LONG

(Verses on page 395)

TURKEY IN THE STRAW

(Verses on page 435)

Parodies:

("We'll All Pull Through" on page 436)
("The Dummy Line" on page 437)
("Tough Luck" on page 438)

THE BELLED BUZZARD

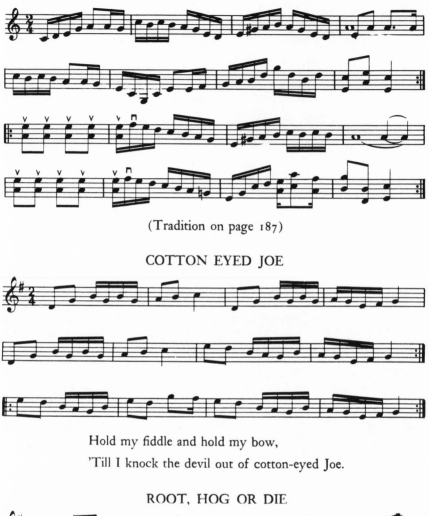

(Tradition on page 187)

COTTON EYED JOE

Hold my fiddle and hold my bow,

'Till I knock the devil out of cotton-eyed Joe.

ROOT, HOG OR DIE

(Verses on page 424)

OLD YALLER HOUN'

Old yaller houn's barkin' treed, up the holler,

It's old mister 'possum, I'll bet half a dollar.

Fetch on the ax, boys, we'll see pretty soon,

He's worth half a dollar if it's old zipp coon.

(Tradition on page 180)

CHEAT OR SWING

DEVIL'S DREAM

Forty days and forty nights
The Devil was a-dreaming.
Around the bark, old Noah's ark,
The rain it was a-streaming.
The monkey washed the baboon's face,
The serpent combed his hair,
And up jumped the Devil
With his pitchfork in the air.

OLD RACCOON

Raccoon's tail got rings all around,
De 'possum's tail am bare.
De rabbit ain't got no tail at all,
Just a little bit a bunch a hair.

EIGHTH OF JANUARY

(Tradition on page 192)

ST. PATRICK'S DAY

CHRISTMAS HORNPIPE

SALLY GOODIN

I had a piece a'pie,

And I had a piece a'puddin',

And I gave it all away,

For to see Sally Goodin.

(Additional verses on page 419)

(Dance call on page 209)

(Tune with violin "discorded," on page 128)

HOP ALONG, SALLY

GOOD NIGHT LADIES

HELL ON THE WABASH

BILLY IN THE LOW LAND

WHEN PAPPY GOES TO TOWN

DARLING CHILD

POLLY WOLLY DOODLE

(Verses on page 420)

TWIN SISTERS

(Dance call on page 209)

THE OLD GREY MARE

The old grey mare, she ain't what she used to be,
Ain't what she used to be, ain't what she used to be.
The old grey mare, she ain't what she used to be,
Many long years ago.

Chorus

Many long years ago.

Many long years ago.

The old grey mare, she ain't what she used to be,

Many long years ago.

67

OPERA REEL

BRING THAT GAL ALONG

FINIS JIG

GOLDEN FLEECE

CIRCASSIAN CIRCLE

(Description of dance on page 215)

DOUG'S FAVORITE
(or Mountain Hornpipe)

MIDNIGHT

FAIRY DANCE

GO TO THE DEVIL AND SHAKE YOURSELF

GREENVILLE.

GREEN GROW THE RUSHES O!

(See also Mexican War tradition on page 184)

GOOD AX ELVE

DIXON'S SLIDE

HULL'S VICTORY

CINCINNATI HORNPIPE

DRUNKEN SAILOR

(Verses on page 389)
("Old Brass Wagon" on page 248)
("Old John Brown Had a Little Indian" on page 448)

BONNIE SWEET BESSIE

DASHING SERGEANT

CANADIAN RIVER

OYSTER RIVER

'POSSUM UP A 'SIMMON TREE

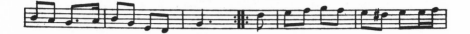

'Possum up a 'simmon tree
Raccoon on the ground.
Raccoon says: "You son-of-a-gun,
Shake them 'simmons down!"

PORTLAND FANCY

(Dance Call on page 213)

THE DOUBLE SHUFFLE

SPEED THE PLOW

DUTCH GIRL

78

THE DEVIL AMONG THE TAILORS

POOR OLD ROBINSON CRUSOE

Poor old Robinson Crusoe was lost,

On an island they say, O,

He stole him a coat from an old billy-goat,

I don't see how he could do so.

(See also song, "Robinson Crusoe" on page 311)

DUSTY SAM

KENDALL'S HORNPIPE

MARCHING MAIDS

POST-OAK GROVE.

JOLLY DOGS

STEAMBOAT QUICKSTEP

LE PETRE'S HORNPIPE

T' OTHER SIDE OF JORDAN

(See also parody "Hoops My Dears" on page 447)

(Verses on page 400)

SNAPPING JIG

JIM CROW

Come, listen, all you gals and boys,
I'm just from Tuckyhoe.
I'm goin' to sing a little song,
My name's Jim Crow.

(Additional verses on page 424)

JACK'S FAVORITE TUNE

JELLY JIG

GARCON VOLANGE

JOHNNY STOLE A HAM

POLLY, PUT THE KETTLE ON

Polly, put the kettle on and slice the bread and butter fine.

Slice enough for eight or nine, we'll all have tea.

(See also "Molly, Put the Kettle On" on page 399)

LAMPLIGHTER'S HORNPIPE

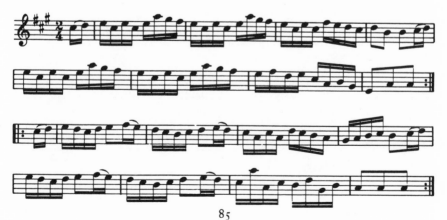

GREY EAGLE

THE WATERFALL

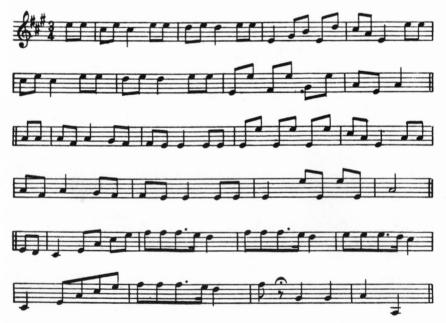

OLE BULL

LONE STAR CLOG

OLD BALL

(Baldy)

There was an ol' hoss,
His name was Ball.
Nothing in the world
Could make him stall.

You'd crack your whip
And cry out: "Ball!"
Out comes wagon,
Team and all.

MELODEON HORNPIPE

SAILORS ON SHORE

JOHNNY QUEEN'S CLOG

OLD TIME CLOG

TENNESSEE REEL

SOLDIER'S DANCE

Fine

D. C.

OLD MOTHER LOGO

INJUN JOHN

TABOUR

SICILIAN CIRCLE

CLUCK, OLD HEN

There are many versions of this tune known as "Cackling Hen."

CACKLING HEN

SIX HAND REEL

OLD KENTUCKY ROAN

ROB ROY

BRICKLAYER'S HORNPIPE

CRADLING RYE

CRIPPLE CREEK

CROWN POINT

COMMENCE YE DARKIES ALL

D.C.

CONSTITUTION HORNPIPE

COONIE IN THE CREEK

JAY BIRD

Jay bird, jay bird, sittin' on a limb,

He winked at me and I winked at him.

I picked up a rock and I hit his shin.

Sez he: "You'd better not do that agin."

GOOD FOR THE TONGUE

JIMMIE JINKS

VENETIAN HORNPIPE

WE WON'T GO HOME TILL MORNING

(See also "We'll All Go Down To Rousers" on page 247)

SUGAR IN THE GOURD

SWALLOW TAIL COAT

STRING TOWN

HUNTSMAN'S HORNPIPE

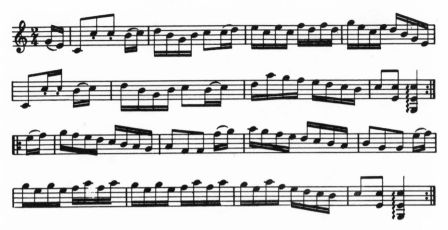

OLD JUBITER

(See also children's play-song, "Old Jubiter," on page 253)

ZARA JIG

MOUNTAIN REEL

D.S.

WILSON'S CLOG

VILLAGE HORNPIPE

HELL AMONG THE YEARLIN'S

JOHNNY MORGAN

(Verses on page 404)

IRISH MILLER

LOUISVILLE HORNPIPE

WALK JAWBONE

Walk, jawbone, Jenny, come along.

In come Sally with her bootees on.

Walk, jawbone, Jenny, come along.

In come Sally with her bootees on.

TILL THE COWS COME HOME

GOLDEN EAGLE

BILLY THE BARBER

NEW LONDON

CLEAR THE KITCHEN

A bull-frog dress'd in soldier's clothes,

    Went out in the field to shoot some crows.

The crows smell powder and fly away.

    That bull-frog mighty mad that day.

(Additional verses on page 407)

THE YANKEE TROT

TICONDEROGA

Fine

D.C. al Fine

KEMO KIMO

In South Car'lina the darkies go

Sing song, Kitty, can't you ki'me, oh!

That's whar the white folks plant the tow,

Sing song, Kitty, can't you ki'me, oh!

(Additional verses on page 418)

(See also another version, "Polly Kimo," on page 450)

GEESE IN THE BOG

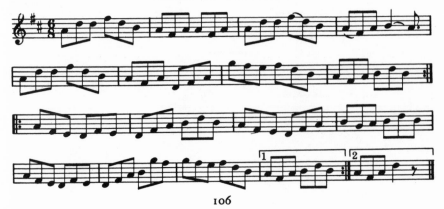

CARRY ME BACK TO OLD VIRGINNY

(See also song on page 346)

BLUE BONNET

OLD TOWSER

Daddy had a bull-dog,
Towser was his name, sir.
He used to chase the bell-cow
Up and down the lane, sir.

He wasn't worth a cuss
For to sick him on a hog, sir.
But whip his weight in wildcats
Could this old bulldog.

VIRGINIA REEL

VINTON'S HORNPIPE

RUNNING FROM THE FEDERALS

WHITE COCKADE

THE CAMPBELLS ARE COMING

(See also, "Campbells are Coming," on page 315)

LANE

(or Scotch No. 2)

PRETTY MAID MILKIN' HER COW

GRANNY PLAYS THE FIDDLE

MELTON'S PARADE

KATY'S RAMBLES

III

MOUNTAIN RANGER

WHEN DARKIES ARE SAD

RED LION HORNPIPE

DEM GOLDEN SLIPPERS

(Verses on page 410)

EVANGELINE

NELSON'S VICTORY

POSSUM CREEK

WEARING OF THE GREEN

(Parody "The Train Pulled in the Station" on page 438)

(See also "Conundrum Song" on page 439)

BONNIE GAY'S REEL

CALEDONIAN HORNPIPE

BILL SIMMONS

115

REDMAN'S REEL

THE GIRL I LEFT BEHIND ME

(Verses on page 417)
(Dance call on page 211)

OLD HICKORY

JOHN SMITH'S HORNPIPE

CONCORDIA

QUINDARO

CANDY GIRL

GARRY OWEN

SANDY HOOK

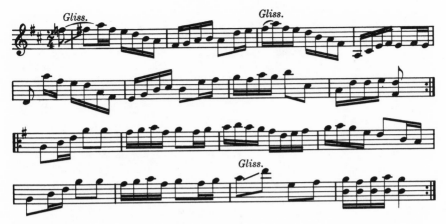

WAIT FOR THE WAGON

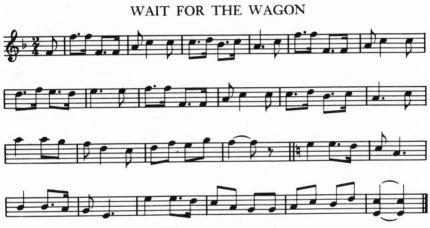

(Verses on page 422)

SLIM GAL

CAPTAIN JINKS

(Verses on page 423)
(Play-party Song "Down the Ohio" on page 423)

120

DOLLY BROWN

FLOP-EARED MULE

("Flop-Eared Mule" is derived from "College Schottisch."
See page 157)

OLD JOE CLARK

(Verses on page 389)

SENECA SQUARE DANCE

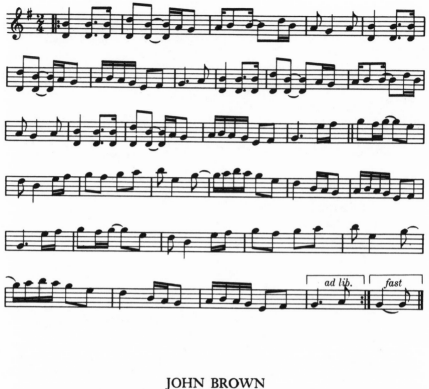

JOHN BROWN

OL' RIDIN' HOSS

A little old man comes a-ridin' by.

Sez I: "Old man, your hoss'll die."

"If he does, I'll tan his skin,

And if he don't, I'll ride 'im agin."

ECHOES FROM THE OZARKS

D.C. ad lib.

THE DEVIL IN A CANEBRAKE

LOST INDIAN

(Tradition on page 185)
(Tune with violin "discorded," on page 128)

BROKEN LANTERN

"I have to 'discord' my fiddle to play that," is a remark often heard at dances when the fiddler is requested to play certain numbers.

The instrument is not really tuned in discord, but in a way which produces a harmonious effect when the bow is drawn across two or more strings at the same time. This manner of tuning also tends to simplify the fingering, as it allows more of the notes to be played on the open strings.

This mode of playing came about by accident, in the opinion of many old-time fiddlers. Beginners, unable to remember the regular method of tuning, learned to play certain tunes in this unusual style. This way was later adopted by other fiddlers and handed down to the present time.

The following tunes are arranged to be played with the fiddle discorded.

Tune Violin

DRUNKEN HICCOUGHS

Fine

pizz.

D.C. al Fine

Rye whiskey, rye whiskey,
Rye whiskey I crave.
If I don't get rye whiskey
I'll go to my grave.

I eat when I'm hungry,
And drink when I'm dry,
And if whiskey don't kill me
I'll live till I die.

Tune Violin

ROSIN THE BOW

Largo

Fine

D.C. al Fine

(See also "Rosin the Bow" on page 392)
(Song "Old Rosin the Beau" on page 57)
(Parody "Paddy's Curiosity Shop" on page 432)

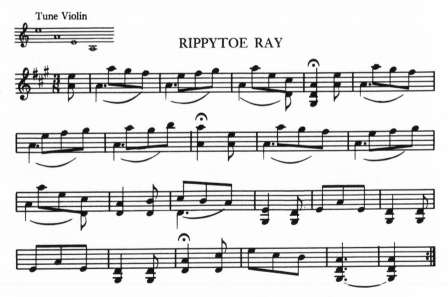

Tune Violin

RIPPYTOE RAY

(See also "Rippytoe Ray" on page 41)

Tune Violin

LOST INDIAN

(See also "Lost Indian" on page 124)

Tune Violin

SALLY GOODIN

(See also "Sally Goodin" on page 64)
(Dance call on page 209)
(Verses on page 419)

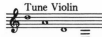

BONAPARTE'S RETREAT

This fiddle-picture of Napoleon at the battle of Waterloo is an old American traditional novelty, which had its origin after the Napoleonic Wars. It is set down here as played on the violin.

Some fiddlers produce startling effects by drumming the strings with the back of the bow, other manipulations simulating musket fire and the general din of battle. *Pizzicato* represents the boom of cannon, while the movement beginning with *Allegro* is played with a continuous bow, to imitate the bagpipes or fife.

The best rendition of this tune the author ever heard was when he arranged the music. The three performers used a violin, a guitar and a pair of steel knitting-needles. The knitting-needles were used as drumsticks, the player striking the strings along the finger-board while the violinist played the tune. The guitar accompaniment was also played with drum effects, similar to those used in the old guitar tune "The Siege of Sebastopol."

ROUND DANCE MUSIC

(Dance instructions on page 227)
Waltzes, Schottisches, Galops, Polkas,
Mazurkas, Varsoviennes and Marches

This round-dance music is written as the old-time fiddlers play it. Many of the numbers are true traditionals and had their origin along with the American square dance tunes.

THE SHENANDOAH WALTZ

CHARLSTON GLIDE WALTZ

SHANTY BOAT WALTZ

STEAMBOAT WALTZ

BLUE HILLS WALTZ

GARLAND WALTZ

IRMA WALTZ

135

THE LAST WALTZ

D.C.

KICK A DUTCHMAN

I'LL BE ALL SMILES TO-NIGHT
(Waltz)

I'll deck my brow with roses,
The loved one may be there.
The gems that others gave me
Will shine within my hair.
And even them that know me
Will think my heart is light.
Though my heart may break tomorrow,
I'll be all smiles tonight.

(Additional verses on page 414)

THE RYE WALTZ

(See also "Pupil's Song" verses on page 443)

137

WHEN THE LEAVES BEGIN TO FALL
(Waltz)

Fine

D.C.

KATE KEARNEY WALTZ

D.C.

D.C.

VALLEY WALTZ

YOU AND I WALTZ
(or Poodle Dog Waltz)

Oh where, oh where has my little dog gone?

Oh where, oh where can he be?

With his tail cut short and his ears cut long,

Oh where, oh where can he be?

My little dog always waggles his tail,

Whenever he wants his grog,

And if the tail were as wise as he,

'Why, the tail would waggle the dog.

My little dog always wags his tail

Whenever I call him to me.

But he's lost himself and he can't be found.

Oh where, oh where can he be?

THE COTILLION

(Description of Dance on page 219)

SHAMUS O'BRIEN
(Waltz)

(See also song, "Shamus O'Brien," on page 405)

ROSE WALTZ

NEWPORT ON THE NARRAGANSETT

(Waltz)

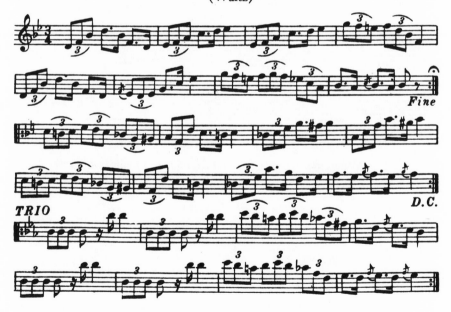

SLEEPY ROBIN WALTZ

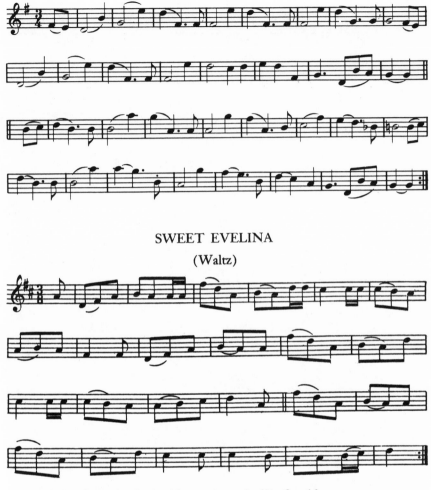

SWEET EVELINA
(Waltz)

Way down in the meadow, where the lily first blows,

Where the wind from the mountain ne'er ruffles the rose,

Lived fond Evelina, the sweet little dove,

The pride of the valley, the girl that I love.

Chorus

Sweet Evelina, dear Evelina,

My love for thee shall never, never die.

(Additional verses on page 403)

OVER THE WAVES

(Waltz)

BROOM WALTZ

(Verses "Buy a Broom," on page 391)

AURORA WALTZ

SI HANKS WALTZ

FIVE STEP WALTZ

Fine

D.C.

MAZOURKAS

FIRST LOVE MAZURKA

D.C.

JENNIE MAZURKA

Fine

D.C.

VARSOVIENNES

VARSOVIENNE

No. 1

D.C.

VARSOVIENNE

No. 2

GALOPS

ROCKIT GALOP

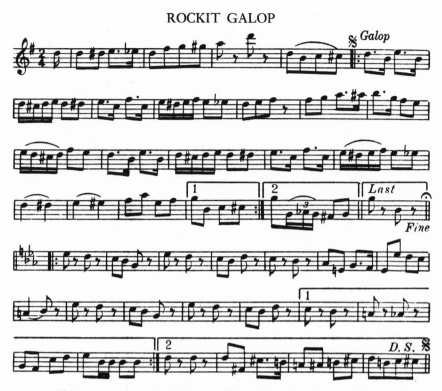

Take partners as for Waltz or Galop. Stand in that position and make a rocking movement. Gent commences with left foot and lady with right. Redowa step, four measures. Glissade to left, four measures. Redowa, four measures. Glissade to right, four measures. Then waltz, galop around the hall and repeat.

PRINCE'S GALOP

D.C. Galop

SCHOTTISCHES

RAINBOW SCHOTTISCHE

MEADOW SCHOTTISCHE

CRYSTAL SCHOTTISCHE

COLLEGE SCHOTTISCHE

(See also "Flop-Eared Mule" on page 121)

SMOKY MOUNTAIN SCHOTTISCHE

D.C.

REDMAN'S FAVORITE SCHOTTISCHE

ROCHESTER SCHOTTISCHE

MILITARY SCHOTTISCHE

MOCKINGBIRD SCHOTTISCHE

ANNIE LAURIE SCHOTTISCHE

D. C.

WOODLAND SCHOTTISCHE

OLD-FASHIONED SCHOTTISCHE

As they marched down this way to the foot of the street,
The band began to play and the music was so sweet.
My heart it was enlisted and I could not get it free,
For the Captain with his whiskers took a sly glance at me.

NOTE: The above verse is reminiscent of Civil War days.

"Old-Fashioned Schottische" was a popular dance number for many years following the Civil War. It is made up from parts of the music of the above-mentioned song and of "Sweet Marie."

(Song "Sweet Marie" on page 379)

POLKAS

HAND ORGAN POLKA

EVERGREEN POLKA

D.C.

SERIOUS POLKA

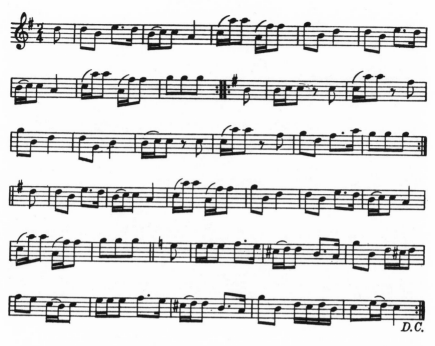

D.C.

HEEL AND TOE POLKA

TRIO

MOUNT VERNON POLKA

D. C.

CON'S FAVORITE POLKA

JENNY LIND'S FAVORITE POLKA

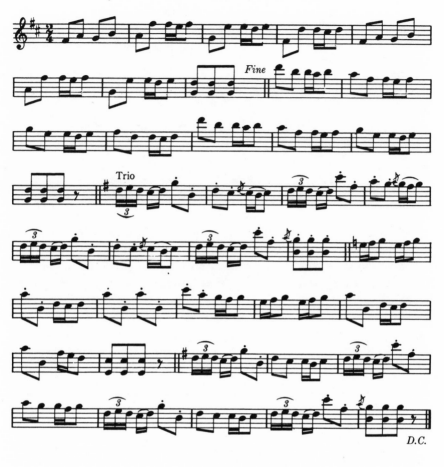

D.C.

Slide two steps forward with the left foot. Execute one Polka step with the left foot. Continue with two more Polka steps, beginning the slide with the right foot and then the left. Change the feet alternately at the beginning of each slide.

HIGH POINT POLKA

OLD WARSAW POLKA

FAIRY POLKA

GORMAN POLKA

D. C.

170

THE BANJO POLKA

SILVER HEELS POLKA

MARCHES

The following marches and quickstep are typical of the early-day American country school Exhibition.

EXHIBITION MARCH NO. 1

EXHIBITION MARCH NO. 2

REVIEW QUICKSTEP

TRADITIONS
OF
AMERICAN FIDDLE TUNES

GREAT BIG TATERS IN SANDY LAND

(Tune on page 39)

From a fiddler who played "Great Big 'Taters in Sandy Land" as his favorite tune, comes the following tradition obtained by the writer thirty years ago. This fiddler was then a man more than seventy years old, who had "larned" the "chune," when a young fellow of twenty, from the "feller" who composed it.

It appears that Steve, the composer, homesteaded 160 acres of land in the rough sandstone hills in a remote section of the county, it being the only land left open for homesteading. Steve was engaged to be married to a beautiful young girl of the community and the wedding was to take place as soon as he developed his farm and got his place built. He broke the new ground, which was all in patches on the tops of the hills, the remainder of the farm consisting of steep rocky hillsides and gullies. As his first crop he planted oats and corn. The oats only came up a few inches and the corn did not even make "nubbins." So the wedding had to be postponed. The boys teased Steve considerably about trying to make a living on the sandy land, but he took it all good-naturedly, as did the girl.

That same year there was a shortage in the potato crop, and, as the land around there was not suitable for potato growing, the farmers had to pay exorbitant prices for the potatoes they had to ship in. Betty, Steve's girl, suggested that he plant potatoes for his next crop. The following spring he planted all his ground accordingly, to the great amusement of his friends. But their amusement was changed to astonishment when that fall Steve harvested 300 bushels to the acre of high grade potatoes and sold them to the farmers at a good price.

The wedding was elaborately celebrated with a big supper, followed by a dance that lasted until morning. This tune, composed by Steve and afterwards played at all the dances, was commonly known as "Steve's Tune," but it was Betty who originated the verses. To get even with those who had "poked fun" at Steve and

his sand farm, she invented the verses, singing them at the dance
that night much to the amusement of the guests.

Sow them oats, but you can't get a stand.

Corn won't grow in that sandy land.

Folks won't think you're much of a man,

If you can't make a livin' on sandy land.

Great big taters in sandy land.

We-all dig 'em out as fast as we can.

The folks all buy 'em from a foolish man,

Raisin' great big taters in sandy land.

NOTE: This is the tune that a certain Senator from Missouri suggested as the state song of that state. Following are some of the
words offered as the lyric:

Ever' time I come to town

The boys keep kickin' my dawg aroun'.

Even effen he is a houn'

They got t' quit kickin' my dawg aroun'.

OLD YALLER HOUN'

(Tune on page 61)

The following sketch was taken down according to family recollections of an old Tennessee fiddler who played "Old Yaller
Houn'" as it was handed down from his "grandpap."

"Back yander in the time of Davie Crockett'n Dan'el
Boone, folks never seed much money. Furs'n pelts, bees-
wax'n taller wuz the legal tender uv the day in the settlement whur we'uns lived.

180

"Most any time when store goods wuz a-runnin' low Pap 'ud say: 'Newt, yew'n Lem go out to the granary'n fotch in all the skins that air dry enough. We'uns air a-goin' over to Bald P'int'n do some tradin' atter dinner.'

"Newt'n Lem 'ud git the skins bundled. Then Pap 'ud say: 'Maw, what d'yew'n Granny need frum the tradin' store?' Maw 'ud more'n likely say: 'Wal, yew mout fotch Granny er box uv snuff. 'N git me a new clay pipe. Be shore to pick as long a stem as yew kin git. Guess that's 'bout all fer the house. Oh yes, git 'nother set o' knit-needles. The yarn's all spun and we'uns'll go to knittin' sox'n mittens next week.' Then Pap 'ud say: 'All right. You'uns tie the hounds up while I git the mule'n we'll ride'n hitch.'

"Come to Bald P'int tradin' post Pap 'ud git th' ol'brown jug filled'n git two horns o' powder'n a pig o' lead'n do tradin' fer Maw'n Granny. There'd most allers be some change left. Maybe a couple o' possum skins'n a weasle or two. Newt'n Lem 'ud trade 'em fer a plug o' flat chawin' terbacker'n we'uns 'ud *ride'n hitch back up th' holler to hum.

"Maybe that night Old Drum 'ud bark treed, up th' holler. Pap 'ud git up'n go outside'n listen fer a spell. Then it 'ud be: 'Fotch the ax, boys, we'll see purty soon. He's wo'th a half-a-dollah ef et's ol' zipp coon.'"

*NOTE: Where two or more people went on a trip together and had but one horse, it was customary to "ride'n hitch." The first "feller" would ride on ahead and hitch the horse to a tree, and start walking on.

When the other parties came to the horse the next "feller" would fork the animal and ride until he overtook the first, and so on, until they reached their destination.

THE WAGONEER

(Tune on page 28)

This tune is a favorite with each generation of fiddlers. The music was not written until the author arranged it as rendered by an old-time fiddler, who had played it at many dances while crossing the plains.

Picture, if you can, a Conestoga freight wagon of the 49's. The rumbling of heavily-ironed wheels and pounding of hoofs upon the rocky trail could be heard long before the four yoke of oxen came into view. The driver, whip in hand, curled the long lash through the air, cracking it over the lumbering oxen in a series of staccato reports like pistol shots as he urged them up the steep trail. At the top was a level plateau overlooking the Missouri, the "Big Muddy River," on which was located the outfitting camp, now the site of Kansas City. On the river bank below was Westport Landing.

Nor was the driver or "wagoneer" expert only at handling many yoke of oxen. He was the best fiddler at the outfitting camp. Led by a spirit of adventure and a desire to conquer the untamed lands of the Great West, bands of pioneers pushed on and on over uncertain trails, through hardships and dangers of which we today can hardly conceive. Yet the night of their arrival at outfitting headquarters found them celebrating the sheer joy of living with a big supper and old-time dance. Here this tune which the wagoneer played so well was always greatly in request, and thus became known as "The Wagoneer," or "Wagner," as it is called today.

YOUNG DAN TUCKER

(Tune on page 55)

Many years ago the writer, with a party of friends, attended a dance back in the hills of the Missouri Ozarks. While hitching the team to a fence there came from the house the strains of an exceedingly vivacious dance tune. As the caller shouted the calls, it was easy to tell by the sounds of the lively shuffling feet that the dancers were "stepping" to the music of one of their favorite tunes.

The fiddlers, two brothers, were accompanied by a bass viol and a guitar. The fiddlers seemed to be playing different tunes, which

182

blended with extraordinary effect. We recognized one as "Old Dan Tucker."

Later, while talking to the fiddlers, we learned that the brothers had created the lead tune some twenty years before, naming it "Young Dan Tucker."

MISSISSIPPI SAWYER

(Tune on page 32)

This tune seems to have a strong appeal among old-time fiddlers. The writer has heard it at old fiddlers' contests from coast to coast. When played by a fiddler who loses himself in the swing of its rhythm, his listeners may hear the faint tinkle of anvils, the clinking of horseshoes and the whetting of sickles and scythes and cradles. It is lively and exciting, yet soothing.

The authorship is credited to an early day sawmill owner, who set up his mill somewhere near the junction of the Ohio and Mississippi rivers. The first enterprise of its kind so far West, it created widespread interest among a people whose only means of producing building materials had been the ax, maul, wedge and rive, and the broadax and adz. Always referred to as "The Mississippi Sawyer," the millwright became a noted character and people congregated daily at his mill from miles around.

It was a tradition among a later generation that the celebration following the test run of the mill was the occasion for a picnic that lasted for days. The picnickers came in covered wagons, well supplied with good things to eat, and pitched camp in the woods near the mill. All hands took part in handling the logs and lumber as the work got under way, and tables and a dance platform were speedily built of the first boards from the saw. After the day's work an open-air banquet was served by the women, and when it was learned that the sawyer was also a fiddler he was immediately chosen by acclamation to play the opening tune of the dance. Thus came into being "The Mississippi Sawyer," one of the rare old tunes of American fiddle lore.

GRINGO

(Tune on page 72)

"Green Grow the Rushes, O!" was a popular melody of American soldiers at the time of the Mexican war, to which they set many verses. The following verse is descriptive of their associations in the land of the señorita:

> Green grow the rushes, O!
>
> Red are the roses, O!
>
> Kiss her quick and let her go,
>
> Before you get the mitten, O!

The deviltry of the American soldier boys was very much resented by the Mexicans. Any American who attempted to kiss a senorita was certain to have his face slapped by her. They called this to "get the mitten." Wherever Americans were would also be heard verses of "Green Grow the Rushes, O!" The Mexicans, in mockery, gave the name "green grow" to their tormentors, their pronunciation being "gringo." After the war "Gringo" became the soubriquet for all Americans.

FORKED DEER

(Tune on page 45)

The old dance tune, "Forked Deer," is easily traceable to the days of powder horns, bullet moulds and coonskin caps.

Like many other very old tunes of American fiddle lore, it had its origin on the isolated frontier and this one has been traced to the first settlers along the Big Sandy River, the border line of **Virginia** and Kentucky.

In the family which preserved this tune, the story, handed down through several generations, credits the authorship to a relative, a noted fiddler of pioneer days. This kinsman was also a famous hunter. There was a spirit of friendly rivalry in the hunt, much the same as there were championships in other lines of activities, and he had established a reputation as a champion deer hunter by always bringing in a forked deer. The forked deer, or two-point buck, was considered the prime venison. As a token of admiration for the hunter as well as the fiddler, his friends set the following words to this popular dance tune which comes down to us as "Forked Deer."

There's the doe tracks and fawn tracks up and down the creek,
  The signs all tell us that the roamers are near.
With the old flint-lock rifle Pappy's gone to watch the lick,
  With powder in the pan for to shoot the forked deer.

THE LOST INDIAN

(Tune on page 124)

A steamboat plying on the Mississippi river anchored at a landing owing to the swollen waters, which were filled with driftwood and logs, making it too difficult to navigate.

One evening, while waiting for the flood waters to subside, the passengers were dancing to the music of a fiddler entertaining them with the tunes and songs of the day. Suddenly, above the sound of the raging river, a quivering wail ending in a series of whoops came eerily across the water, and out of the impenetrable darkness into the radius of the boat's light floated a great log. On it was an Indian struggling to keep his balance. The wild cry echoed once again over the river and then the swirling currents caught the log, and the unfortunate redskin disappeared in a mighty plunge under the boiling waters.

This tragedy made such a lasting impression on the fiddler's mind that he later became mildly insane. Thereafter the only tune that he would play was the one interrupted by this harrowing experience, in which he incorporated the wails and shouts of the lost Indian.

PUNCHEON FLOOR

(Tune on page 57)

"Puncheon Floor" has been handed down as one of the favorite old dance tunes of America. More than any other of the traditional tunes of the olden days it seems to carry the spirit of sociability of the folks "back yonder," where the people of a community were then closely banded together in a social order based upon the greatest good of the greatest number.

The homes were built of logs and shingled with clap-boards. The floors were made of puncheons, split logs laid with the round side down. After the puncheons were edged with the broad-ax and joined together, the floor was surfaced and smoothed off with an adz until it was as smooth as a modern dance floor. It was thus that this old tune had its genesis.

Vision, if you can, a picture of that early period of the nation's history. A big log house in a grove of stately trees of the virgin forest, surrounded by granaries and barns filled with a bountiful harvest. It is evening. As the moon rises over the distant wooded hills the jolly revelers begin to arrive from near and far, for this is to be the first dance of the season. Above the sounds of gaiety and light-hearted banter can be heard the tones of the violins as the fiddlers tune up, and the voice of the floor manager calling: "One more couple here —one more couple!" Then, as the set is filled, a word to the musicians: "All right! Let 'er go!"

The strains of "Puncheon Floor" go bounding and echoing out across the valley as the caller shouts: "Honor your partners and the lady on the left! Join hands and circle to the left! Balance all!

186

Swing your partners! Left Alemand! Once and a Half and Right and Left Grand!

THE BELLED BUZZARD

(Tune on page 60)

Back of the old fiddle tune, "The Belled Buzzard," is a tradition which had its origin in the Ozark mountains. The story concerns a settlement along a river bottom. One bank of the river was bordered for miles by high unscaleable bluffs crowned with scrub timber, the home and breeding place of thousands of buzzards.

Hog raising was the main source of income of the community. Mast from the acorn-bearing trees furnished food for the droves of hogs ear-marked and turned into the woods each year, to be rounded up in the fall ready for market.

One summer hog cholera broke out among the porkers. The buzzards, feasting on the dead carcasses, carried the disease from one section of the country to another. There was an unwritten law that these birds should not be killed, but the farmers were aware that, unless some action was taken to check the spread of the disease, their hogs, together with their incomes, would be wiped out entirely.

A meeting was called. It was decided to capture one of the birds and fasten a small sheep bell to it, in the hope that it would cause them to leave. One of the birds was accordingly trapped and belled. His arrival among the others created a great commotion and in a few days the flock of buzzards disappeared, only the belled buzzard remaining. Finally he, too, took flight.

At the end of the summer there was an epidemic of typhoid fever in the community, many dying. About that time the belled buzzard reappeared, the tinkle of his bell being plainly heard as he soared above the houses. He came and went time after time and always following his reappearance some sort of calamity happened. The return of the belled bird aroused apprehension in the

187

minds of the more superstitious and his presence became associated with their misfortunes. They believed the repulsive fowl was possessed of an evil spirit. Many believe he still roams the skies, as he has for more than a hundred years, so that even today any report of the belled buzzard casts a spell of gloom over them.

The tune, "The Belled Buzzard," has been handed down through the years with this tradition, the plucking of the fiddle string in certain places in the music representing the tinkle of his bell.

STEP TO THE MUSIC, JOHNNY

(Tune on page 58)

During the Civil War, a foraging party of Northern troops came upon a dance attended by a large body of Confederate soldiers. Surrounding the place and taking them by surprise, the invaders captured the Southerners without a shot being fired. The fiddler, not a soldier although a strong Southern sympathiser, became somewhat sarcastic in his remarks to the Northerners, so they decided to take him along with the other prisoners.

One of the Yankees conceived the idea of having the fiddler play a lively tune to march by on their way back to the Northern lines. So, at the bayonet's point, the fiddler obeyed. From time to time the Yankees would yell: "Step to the music, Johnny!" which subsequently became the accepted name for this tune.

ARKANSAW TRAVELER

(Tune on page 46)

Perhaps the most widely known and best remembered of the old fiddle tune traditions is the one of the "Arkansaw Traveler." It is given here as the writer heard it "acted out" many years ago at a school "exhibition." This was in the days when it was the custom of the "destrict" school to entertain the community with

188

the said exhibition following the last day of the school term. That is, a stage was built and equipped with sliding curtains. The kerosene lamps were all trimmed and their reflectors brightened. An organ was hauled in by one of the patrons who happened to have one, and, after a few days rehearsing of the dialogues, speeches, songs and music, the show was ready to go on.

CHARACTERS

ARKANSAWER........... A native of Arkansas.

TRAVELER.............. A tourist.

GINNIE............... The Arkansawers daughter.

Voices representing the Arkansawer's

sons, Newt and Rufus.

SCENE

Arkansawer seated in front of his cabin home, playing the *"coarse" part of "Arkansaw Traveler." He plays throughout the skit, except for interruptions during his conversation with the traveler. He fiddles from two to four measures of the tune each time, picking up the next measure where he left off.

Sound of horses approaching. Rider is singing "My Boyhood Happy Days Down on the Farm."

ARKANSAWER. (Stops playing and listens, then calls to his daughter). "Ginnie, hyer comes a Federal."
GINNIE. (From behind left wing). "Reckon it air, pap."

* Nearly all of the old fiddle tunes have but two parts, designated by old-time fiddlers as the "coarse" and "fine." The coarse part represents that movement played principally on the D and G strings. The fine part is that which is played on the A and E strings.

189

TRAVELER. (Later, from behind right wing). "Hello there, my friend."

ARKANSAWER. "Howdy, stranger."

TRAVELER. (Entering). "What would be the chance to get a drink?"

ARKANSAWER. (Calling to daughter). "Ginnie, go round to ther spring'nd fotch ther stranger a gourd uv water." (Plays first four bars of tune slowly).

GINNIE. (Bringing gourd across stage to right wing). "Hyer ye air, stranger."

TRAVELER. "Thanks." (Jovially) "Say, I've heard there's some mighty good moonshine in this part of the country. Maybe you can tell me where I could find a snort."

ARKANSAWER. (Sarcastically) "Stranger, ef'n you'uns'll jist foller yan path down that 'ar holler thar, hit'll take yer right down to a still, ef'n that's what you'uns air a-lookin' fur. And ther Combs boys'll be thar a-cookin' off some uv ther best co'n licker ever made."

TRAVELER. "That's fine. I'll just leave my horse and traveling bag here till I get back."

ARKANSAWER. (Mildly). "You'uns don't need to go a-worryin' 'bout ther hoss 'er airy satchel." (Darkly) "Ef'n yer goes down thar you'uns ain't a-comin' back." (Plays next two bars of tune).

TRAVELER. "Ahem, I see. You think I'm a revenue officer."

ARKANSAWER. (In a low voice). "We'uns don't take time ter do much thinkin' when them 'ar kind of fellers air around hyer." (Plays last two bars of the tune vigorously, ending with a flourish).

TRAVELER. "I see there's a big hole in the roof of your house — looks as if you'd started to fix it. Why didn't you finish the job?"

ARKANSAWER. "Rained so hard I couldn't."

TRAVELER. "But it isn't raining now."

ARKANSAWER. "When hit ain't a-rainin' hit don't need fixin." (Plays first two bars of tune).

TRAVELER. "Does this road go to Little Rock?"

ARKANSAWER. "Stranger, I've lived hyer all my life and I hain't ever seen hit go thar yit. But ef'n you'uns air a-lookin' fur rocks, thar's a helluva big 'un right down 'ar in my pasture." (Plays next two bars of tune).

TRAVELER. "Say, if you would get it out of your head that I'm a Federal man, I'd like to stay all night with you folks."

ARKANSAWER. (Plays next two bars with a flourish).

TRAVELER. "Can't you play the other part of that tune?"

ARKANSAWER. "I ain't ever hyerd airy other part to hit."

TRAVELER. "Let me see your fiddle." (Plays both parts of "Arkansaw Traveler" through, several times, very lively).

ARKANSAWER. (Excitedly). "Wal, wal, now, stranger, ef'n yer can put up with what we'uns have, I'd be proud fur yer ter stay all night — er stay as long as yer wants to." (Calls to his boys). "Newt, yew take that 'ar hoss to ther barn 'nd feed 'im six ye'rs uv co'n 'nd a gallon uv oats. Rufus, yew tote ther stranger's satchel in."

VOICES OF NEWT AND RUFUS. "All right, pap." (Sound of horse being led away).

WOMAN'S VOICE. (From behind curtain). "Pap, ef'n you'uns air a-fixin' ter play some chunes ye'd better git started afore hit gits too dark ter see. Ther houns' got inter ther candles this atternoon 'nd et 'em all up. Turn them 'ar chickens, too, afore yer fergit it, pap!"

TRAVELER. "What does she mean by 'turn the chickens?'"

ARKANSAWER. "Now, stranger, I got a-hankerin' ter hyer you'uns play some chunes on ther fiddle." (Stops as he realizes that traveler has spoken to him). "Ther chickens? Wal, yer see, stranger, a pole-cat ketched ther ol' speckled hen 'nd ther young 'uns raised her chickens by hand out thar in ther shed. Now ther little critters got big enough so's they roost up on ther rim uv ther meal barr'l." (Calls) "Ginnie, fotch out yer dulcimer!"

GINNIE. "All right, pap. Jist as soon as I he'p Ma put ther young-'uns ter bed."

(Enter Ginnie with dulcimer).

191

They play several tunes. The Arkansawer calls out the title each time before they play.

ARKANSAWER. "Now, stranger, play that'n we'uns played when you'uns fust got hyer."

TRAVELER. "Oh yes, you mean the one I improvised a "fine" part to." (Plays the tune. Arkansawer keeps time by stomping his feet vigorously).

ARKANSAWER. "Stranger, what do yer call that chune?"

TRAVELER. "Well, I guess we'll have to call that the 'Arkansaw Traveler.' "

ARKANSAWER. "Hit shore air a good'n. Wal, good-night, stranger."

TRAVELER. "Good-night, folks."

(CURTAIN)

EIGHTH OF JANUARY

(Tune on page 63)

The old fiddle tune, "Eighth of January," was formerly known as "Jackson's Victory." It was so named in commemoration of Andrew Jackson and his frontiersmen at the Battle of New Orleans, January 8, 1815. Here, cornered in a swamp, greatly outnumbered and poorly equipped, these fearless pioneers fought and won the last military engagement in the War of 1812.

Like many other old traditional fiddle tunes, it was played as a march on the fife and drums at recruiting stations in the North during the Civil War. For political reasons the title may have been changed at that time to "Eighth of January." However, in a few instances, the writer still found it called "Jackson's Victory."

OLD MOLLY HARE

(Tune and verse on page 30)

The tune "Old Molly Hare" is much older than the verse accompanying it. The writer got the tradition of the verse from a man who had been a noted caller of old-time dances, in his younger days. His family came from Virginia about 1870, taking up land in the prairie country of south-west Missouri and south-eastern Kansas with other settlers. At that time, the country abounded in prairie chickens, quail, rabbits and numerous other small game. Rabbits, especially, were so abundant that they were considered a nuisance, cattle being frequently crippled by stepping into rabbit burrows when being herded; or a horse would break its leg in the same manner, when being ridden at top speed to head off a runaway steer.

The origin of the verse, in which "Old Molly Hare" is found digging out a post hole, came about when settlers first began to fence in their pasture lands. Digging post holes is arduous work. Spaced along the line of fencing, the settlers would often find many rabbit burrows which could be enlarged and used to place a post in at a great saving of labor. Rabbits burrow into the ground quite deeply where the terrain is soft, lining their nests with their own fur when preparing for their young, and banking the earth around the opening to shed the rainwater.

As a matter of pride, settlers took great pains to have their posts carry a straight line of fence. However, there was one much-loved, easy-going character in the community, whose ingenious efforts to avoid over-exertion were a constant source of amusement to his friends and neighbors. When he built his fence he was not particular about a straight line. He selected rows of rabbit holes, set his posts, strung the wire and had his fencing done in no time at all. But the result was even more erratic than he had anticipated. He was surveying the completed work one day when several neighbors, coming in from the range, rode up. They took one look at the fence and then had their usual laugh, to poor old John's embarrassment.

"John," said one, in a voice of suppressed amusement, "how much liquor does it take to the mile, to build a fence like that?"

"Well," said John, scratching his head, "I hadn't calc'lated fer it to be a worm fence. Reckon, though, if I had a still hitched to it and the neighbors pourin' cold water along, like they do on all my honest endeavors, you fellers 'ud be down at t'other end of the fence holdin' yer cups to ketch the whiskey!"

As soon as the laughter had subsided over John's turning the tables, the neighbor added: "Anyhow, you certainly did get your fencing done in a hurry, John. Did you have any help?"

"Yes and no," was the reply. "I sort of took advantage of Mother Nature on part of the work. Old Molly Hare dug the post holes — but me and the mules had to set the posts and string the wire!"

It was shortly after this episode that the above-mentioned verse appeared, and began to be used by callers when the tune "Old Molly Hare" was played.

TRADITIONAL CALLS

OF

THE AMERICAN SQUARE DANCE

The figures of the American square dance as it developed in rural pioneer America are not measured in bars of music. The dancers follow no dancing master's rules. When the set is filled with the required number of couples, the caller gives the musicians their cue and the dancers begin as the caller gives the first call: "Honor your partner! Lady on the left! All join hands and circle left!" By the time the dancers have reached their original places, they have all found steps in time to the rhythm of the music and the dance continues until the caller completes the figures of the set and whistles a signal to the musicians to stop.

INSTRUCTIONS FOR CALLING IN SQUARE DANCES

To become a good caller the first requisite is that the voice be pitched to harmonize with the music.

For "the first couple out," or the head of the set, the caller should choose a couple who are familiar with the figures he intends to call. Any beginners in the set should be the last couples to go round. This will give them an opportunity to acquaint themselves with the figures, by watching the other dancers. This arrangement is essential. Where the caller is serving more than one set at a time, a mistake in any one set can throw the others into confusion.

A caller may prolong the set, as the case may be, by using a "final call" after each couple have completed their round, or by calling, in the Grand Right and Left, "Once and a Half and Right and Left back," or "Once and a Half and keep hooking on." Or, if he desires to shorten the time he can call only a simple Grand Right and Left to the Promenade.

Where there are two or more sets on the floor and the caller wishes to combine them for the final Grand Right and Left, this call may be used: "Balance home! Attention all! General Grand Right and Left around the hall! When you come to your partners Promenade all!" The execution of these calls requires some time. During this period the caller may "do his stuff" by filling in with humorous calls, such as: "Chase the 'possum, chase the coon! Chase that purty gal round the room! Swing grandma, swing grandpa! Swing that gal from Arkansaw!" and others. The performance ends with the call "Promenade to your seats!"

EXPLANATION OF TERMS USED

HONOR YOUR PARTNER! To make a bow or curtsey.
ALAMANDE LEFT! Gents turn ladies on the left and return to partners.
GRAND RIGHT AND LEFT! Hands right and left around the

197

set until partners meet. Ladies move to the left and gents to the right.

PROMENADE! Join crossed hands with partner, right hands above the left, and march around to place.

DO-SE-DO! (Dos-a-Dos). After four hands around gents change right hand for left and turn partners. They pass each other to the right and turn the opposite lady with right hand. Then pass each other to the left and return to partners. Swing partner with both hands joined.

DO-SE-DO AND A LITTLE MORE DO! Double do-se-do.

LADIES CHAIN! Ladies cross over to opposite gentlemen, passing each other to the left. Swing gents once around with left hands. Return to partners, passing to left of each other and turn partners with left hand.

HALF PROMENADE! Join hands as in Promenade. Cross to opposite side of set. Disengage hands and join hands, gents right and ladies left, and return to place.

RIGHT AND LEFT THROUGH! Head and foot couples (or side couples) join hands and cross over to opposite side of set. On meeting in center they disengage hands. Ladies pass between gents. Gents take ladies left hands in their left. Ladies turn around gents toward outside of set. Gents change right hands for left.

FORWARD AND BACK! Four steps forward and four steps backward. Same for one person, one couple, or all.

BALANCE TO THE CORNERS! Turn and face corner. Take four steps forward and four steps backward, passing on the left. Swing corner with both hands. Return to place, stepping backward.

CHASSE! (Sashay). Any movement where hands are not joined.

BALANCE ALL! Execute any few steps before swinging partners.

ROQUET! Two couples join hands with partners. Each couple circles around other couple. Or three couples form two sets of three people joining hands. Each set circles around other set. Or four couples form two sets of four people joining hands. Each set circles around other set.

WHEEL PROMENADE! Inside gents or ladies link arms with

partners and join hands with opposites across set. Then turn right or left, as the call may require.

ONCE AND A HALF AND RIGHT AND LEFT BACK!
Meet partners, swing Once and a half, then Right and Left back in opposite directions until partners meet again.

ORNAMENTAL CALLS

Following are some of the ornamentations used by callers to enliven the dance:

"Powder River!"
Same as "Balance All!" Each person executes steps before swinging partner. The caller may shout: "Powder River!" at any time during the Grand Right and Left. The dancers pause, cut the pigeonwing, dance a jig, or execute some special steps before swinging partners.

*   *   *

"Swing that gal like swinging on a gate! Meet your partner and Promenade Eight!"
Used in ending Grand Right and Left.

*   *   *

"Honor your partners right and wrong! Join hands and circle along! Like the whoopin' crane when the shitepoke said: 'We must get a little rain, the creeks are low and the ponds all dry! If it wasn't for the tadpoles we'd all die!'

"Balance All! Swing your partners! Left Alemand! Turn to your partners and Right and Left Grand! Promenade All!"
May be used as the preliminary call beginning any set.

*   *   *

"Sow them oats and plant that corn! Once and a Half and keep a-hookin' on!"

Used in double Grand Right and Left.

* * *

"The pee-a-wee whistles and the jaybirds sing! Meet your partner with the elbow swing and Promenade on to the end of the ring!

Used in ending the Grand Right and Left to the Promenade.

* * *

"Balance home! Swing your partners! Left Alamand! Once and a Half and Right and Left Grand!

> "As I was a-goin' down the road,
>
> I met Miss Possum and I met Mr. Toad.
>
> And every time the toad would sing,
>
> The 'possum cut the pigeonwing."

At the caller's words, "cut the pigeonwing," dancers pause while ladies execute steps of a jig before swinging partners.

Used when the tune "Turkey in the Straw" is played for the set.

* * *

"Squaw in the canebrake, papoose on her back! When you meet that Injun, take a back track!"

Same as Once and a Half and Right and Left back.

* * *

"Buckskin moccasin on a puncheon floor! Swing Once and a Half and then some more!"
Swing Once and a Half and repeat. Then Right and Left on.

* * *

"The bullfrog warbled some meadowlark songs, and he got the epizootic in his get-alongs! Give 'im a crutch and give 'im a spade! Limp along, dig along, Promenade!"
Used in double Grand Right and Left.

* * *

"Four yoke of oxen to a mould-board plow! You can turn square corners if you know how!"
Square Promenade, as in reels.

* * *

"Cradle that wheat and cradle that rye! Buckwheat batter and huckleberry pie! Gingerbread pudding and brandy mincemeat! Promenade around until you find a seat!"
The last Promenade, ending the set.

* * *

"Spin that yarn and weave that jeans! She's as purty a little gal as ever you seen! Don't swing 'er round the waist cause she smiles at you! For you'll get the mitten just as sure as you do!"
Used in double Grand Right and Left.
The "waist swing" was taboo, but occasionally some bold swain would attempt it. "Get the mitten" meant that a girl had jilted her beau. Sometimes it meant a slap in the face, if the breach of manners justified it.

* * *

"Grand Right and Left till you hear the next call! You won't meet your honey till away next fall! When you go a-courtin' don't stay too late! Just hitch your hoss at the old brown gate! When ma says: 'Bootjack, Nancy, thar he goes, or you'll eat your johnny-cake a-standin' on your toes! Do your sparkin' but don't be late!' Meet your partners and Promenade Eight!"

* * *

"Hogs in the tater patch, chunk 'em through the gate! When you come to your partners Promenade Eight!"

* * *

"Boys, go a-runnin' to that purty little maid! Swing 'er like you love 'er and all Promenade!"

* * *

SQUARE DANCE CALLS

QUADRILLES

The Beginner's Set

The Preliminary and Final Calls given in the "Beginner's Set" are also used for beginning and ending sets where the words "(Preliminary Call)" and "(Final Call)" are printed.

Preliminary Call

Honor your partners and the lady on the left!
All join hands and circle to the left!

Balance All!

Swing your partners! Left Alamand! Once and a Half and Right and Left Grand!

Promenade All!

Figure

The first couple out to the couple on the right! Four hands around!

> Ladies Do-se-do, and gents, you know!
> Balance to the next couple!
>
> Four hand around!
> Ladies Do-se-do, and gents, you know!
> Balance to the next couple!
>
> Four hands around!
> Ladies Do-se-do, and gents, you know!
> Balance to the next couple!
>
> Four hands around and away you go!
> Do-se-do, and a little more do!
> Balance home and balance all!

Final Call

Swing your partners! Left Alamand! Once and a Half and Right and Left Grand!

Promenade All!

Repeat the Figure, including the Final Call, with "Next couple out to the couple on the right," until all couples have been around the set. Use the same rule in all the following patterns.

THE STAR

Preliminary Call (See "The Beginner's Set")

Figure

First couple out to the couple on the right! Form a star with right hands crossed and turn to the right!

Turn right back with the left hands crossed!
Break the star and four hands around!
Ladies Do, and gents, you know!
Balance to the next couple!

First couple repeats same figure with remaining two couples.

Final Call (See "The Beginner's Set")

Dance continues until all four couples have performed the figure.

LADY ROUND THE LADY

Preliminary Call (See "The Beginner's Set")

Figure

First couple out to the couple on the right!
Lady round the lady and the gent, solo!
Lady round the gent, but the gent don't go!
Four hands around and away you go!
Ladies Do and gents, you know!
Balance to the next couple!

First couple repeats same figure with remaining two couples.

Final Call (See "The Beginner's Set")

Dance continues until all four couples have performed the figure.

ROQUET SIX AND EIGHT

Preliminary Call (See "The Beginner's Set")

Figure

First couple balance to the center and swing!
Lady to the first couple, gent to the next!
With three hands around and Roquet six!
Break and circle with six hands around!
Balance Six!
Swing your partners and Right and Left Six!
Wheel Promenade!
First couple balance to the last couple here!
Four hands there and four hands here, and Roquet eight when you get straight!
Break and circle eight with eight hands around!
Swing your partners! Alamande Left and Grand Right and Left!
Wheel Promenade!

Final Call (See "The Beginner's Set")

Dance continues until all four couples have performed the figure.

CAST OFF SIX, FOUR AND TWO

Preliminary Call (See "The Beginner's Set")

Figure

First couple balance and swing!
Chasse down the center and back!
Down the center and cast off six! The lady to the right and the gent to the left! Down the outside and back to place!
Swing the girl that you adore! Down the center and cast off four!
Swing once more! Down the center and cast off two, and that will do!

Everybody swing! Alamande Left! Once and a Half and Grand Right and Left!

Promenade All!

Dance continues until all four couples have performed the figure.

BIRD IN THE CAGE

Preliminary Call (See "The Beginner's Set")

Figure

First couple out to the couple on the right! Lady in the center with three hands around!

Lady steps out and gent steps in! Three hands around and circle again!

The crow hops out and four hands around!

Ladies Do, and gents, you know!

All balance to the next couple! Bird in the cage with five hands around!

The bird hops out and the crow hops in! Join five hands and circle again!

The crow hops out and six hands around!

Balance six!

Swing your partners! Alamande Left and Right and Left Six!

Six Promenade!

Catch the last two birds on the fourth little mound! Put the birdie in the cage and seven hands around!

Let the birdie hop out and the crow hop in! Join hands and circle again!

The crow hops out no more to roam! All flap your wings and circle home!

Final Call (See "The Beginner's Set")

Dance continues until all four couples have performed the figure.

206

CHEAT OR SWING

Preliminary Call (See "The Beginner's Set")

Figure

First couple balance and swing!
First lady balance to the gent on the right!
Swing him if you please, or cheat him if you like!
On to the next! He won't be mad! If you cheat him
he'll be sorry, if you swing him he'll be glad!
On to the next! His girl won't care! Swing him if you
will, or cheat him if you dare!
Balance home, little girl, and everybody swing! Once
and a Half like swinging on a gate! Alamande Left and Right
and Left Eight!
Promenade!

Repeat the call for each lady in the set.

Other bantering calls are: "Swing him if you love him,
or cheat him if you don't!"
"Here's the last one, standing in the shade! If you don't
swing him you'll be an old maid!"

OLD DAN TUCKER

(Tune "Old Dan Tucker" on page 55)

Form a circle of four or more couples. In center are one or
more "Tuckers" (gents), without partners.

Figure

Balance all to Old Dan Tucker!
Swing your partners! Alamande Left! Once and a Half
and Grand Right and Left! (Tuckers join in the right and left).
All Promenade! (Tuckers remain in the center)

All join hands and Forward and Back!

Circle to the Left!

Swing your partners! Left Alamand! Once and a Half and Right and Left Grand!

Repeat as often as desired.

THE GRAPEVINE

Preliminary Call (See "The Beginner's Set")

Figure

First couple out to the couple on the right!

Four hands around and Do-se-do!

Join four hands in a row! Go through those arches and around to the right! (Couples, in turn, raise joined hands to form arches while the first gent leads through)

Pick up the next couple and six hands around!

Balance Six!

Swing your partners and join that row! First gent leads wherever you go! Through those arches one by one! Pick up the next couple when you are done, and circle eight when you get straight!

Balance Eight!

Swing your partners and join that line for the grapevine twist! Through those arches like a winding snake, and don't you let that grapevine break! Lead to the right and balance eight when you get straight!

Final Call (See "The Beginner's Set")

Dance continues until all four couples have performed the figure.

This is a long change. Sometimes, by agreement between the dancers and the caller, only two or three couples go through it.

TWIN SISTERS

(Tune "Twin Sisters," on page 67)

Preliminary Call (See "The Beginner's Set")

First two ladies join hands, accompanied by first two gentlemen, and chasse down center and back to place. First two
gents join hands, accompanied by first two ladies on outside,
and chasse down center and back to place. First couple chasse
down center and back, then chasse down center, cast off right
and left, and return to place.

Final Call (See "The Beginner's Set")

Dance continues with second two couples performing the
figure.

SALLY GOODIN

(Tune "Sally Goodin," on page 64)

Preliminary Call

Honor your partners and the lady on the left!
All join hands and circle to the left!

Caller sings verse:

I had a piece a'pie,

And I had a piece a'puddin',

And I gave it all away,

For to see Sally Goodin.

Balance All!
Swing your partners Once and a Half, and Right and
Left on!

209

Swing grandpa! Swing grandma! Swing that gal from Arkansaw! Come on, boys, don't be afraid! Swing Sally Goodin and all Promenade!

Figure

The first Sally balance and swing Jimmy Riddle!

(her partner).

Now, Jimmy swing Sally and leave her in the middle, and balance to the right-hand couple! With three hands around like lambs in the valley! You swing his girl while he swings Sally! (i. e. after three hands around, Jimmy swings second gent's girl, while *he* swings Sally).

Balance to the next! Three hands you whirl! Let the gent swing Sally and you swing his girl! (i.e. after three hands around, Jimmy swings third gent's girl, while *he* swings Sally)

On to the last three hands you roam! Same old swing! Then everybody swing! Now take Sally home! (i.e. after three hands around, Jimmy swings fourth gent's girl while *he* swings Sally. Then other three gents swing partners, while Jimmy swings Sally home)

Final Call

Balance All!

Swing Sally Goodin and Left Alamand! Swing Sally once more and Right and Left Grand!

Come on, boys, don't be afraid! Meet Sally Goodin and all Promenade!

Dance continues until all four Sallies (ladies) have performed the figure.

DOWN EAST BREAKDOWN

Figure

Eight hands around! All Right and Left! Ladies Chain! All

Forward and Back! Forward again and pass on to the next! Every other couple raise their hands! Other couples stoop and pass through!

Turn around at each end of the set! Balance All! Swing your partners! Left Alamand! Once and a Half and Right and Left Grand! Promenade All!

Repeat figure four times.

THE GIRL I LEFT BEHIND ME

(Tune "The Girl I Left Behind Me" on page 116)

Form a set of six couples. Ladies on one side, gents opposite. The head couple cross over to couple at foot.

Figure

First couple with the second lady down the center! And leave that girl behind them! (They leave second lady in center at head).

Back to place! Now take that gent to the pretty little girl, the girl you left behind you! (They take second gent to second lady).

Back to place! (First and second couples). Down the center and both couples back to place! And right and left four at the head of the set!

Dance continues until all couples have performed the figure.

Final Call (See "The Beginner's Set")

FORWARD SIX AND RIGHT AND LEFT FOUR

Preliminary Call (See "The Beginner's Set")

Figure

First three couples forward and back! All swing partners half around! Forward Six and back again! Swing partners to places!

First couple go below second couple and Right and Left Four! Balance All! Swing your partners! Alamande Left and Grand Right and Left! All Promenade!

Dance continues until all couples have performed the figure.

Final Call (See "The Beginner's Set")

SQUARE EIGHT

Preliminary Call (See "The Beginner's Set")

Figure

First four Forward and Back! Side four the same! First four swing with partners! Side four the same! Ladies to the center with right hands across! Turn to the right and Balance back to place! Gents to the center and hands across! Balance back to place! Ladies to the center with four hands around, and Balance back to place!

All hands around to the right! Right hand to partner and Grand Right and Left! Balance All! Swing partners! Balance to corners! Swing corners! Swing partners and single Promenade! Balance All! Swing partners! Balance to corners! Swing corners! Back to your partners and swing! Promenade All!

Dance continues until all six couples have performed the figure.

Final Call (See "The Beginner's Set")

OLD CALIFORNIA

Preliminary Call (See "The Beginner's Set")

Figure

All Chasse to the right! Half Balance! Chasse and swing Four, half around! Chasse to the right! Half Balance! Chasse and swing four to places! Ladies Chain!

Balance All! Swing partners! Swing Four, half around and back! Half Promenade! Half Right and Left! All forward and back! Forward and cross to face the next couple!

Repeat figure four times.

Final Call (See "The Beginner's Set")

PORTLAND FANCY

(Tune on page 77)

Preliminary Call (See "The Beginner's Set")

Figure

Head couple down the center, and foot couple up the outside! (At the same time) Meet partners and swing! Head couple down the outside, and foot couple up the center!
Ladies Chain at the head of the set, and Right and Left at the foot! Right and Left at the head of the set, and Ladies Chain at the foot! All Forward and Back! Forward and cross by opposite couples and face the next four!

Repeat figure four times.

Final Call (See "The Beginner's Set")

LADIES TRIUMPH

Preliminary Call (See "The Beginner's Set")

Figure

First lady join hands with second gent! Down the center! First gent go down after them! Take partner by the left hand

and join hands with the other gent, behind the lady's back, and up the center to place! First gent and second lady down the center!

First lady goes after them, and up the center as before! First couple down the center and back! Down the center and cast off! Lady to the right and gent to the left! Up the outside and back to place!

Final Call (See "The Beginner's Set")

Dance continues until all couples have performed the figure.

OYSTER RIVER

Preliminary Call (See "The Beginner's Set")

Figure

First couple cross the set! Go between the second and third couples facing out from the set! Join hands and balance three on a side! Swing the right-hand person! Balance again! Swing the left-hand person!

Swing partner with the right hand half around! Down the center and back! Down the center and cast off! With the lady to the right and gent to the left, and back to place!

Final Call (See "The Beginner's Set")

Dance continues until all couples have performed the figure.

MONEY MUSK

(Tune "Money Musk" on page 52)

Form set of six couples. Ladies on one side, gents opposite. Ladies' right is the head of the set.

214

Figure

Head couple swing Once and a Half! Go between the second and third couples and forward six!

Swing three-quarters around! Forward six again! Swing three-quarters around! Right and Left Through, and Right and Left back!

Repeat figure four times.

Circassian Circle

(Tune "Circassian Circle" on page 70)

Form a circle with eight couples, in sets of two couples facing each other.

Figure

Hands across set and turn partners!
Ladies Chain!
Promenade once around and across to the next couple!

All must commence at once. At the conclusion of the figure couples in original sets pass each other and repeat figure with neighbor couples. Continue until original partners meet.

Polka on the Corners

Form a set with eight couples. Head couples 1st, couples on the right 3rd, foot couples 2nd and last couples 4th.

Preliminary Call (See "The Beginner's Set")

First Figure Ladies at the head give right hands and turn! Left hands to partners and turn! Lead couples polka! Turn corners! All polka! (Sides the same)

Second Figure First couple polka! Ladies Chain! All polka! (Repeat with third, second and fourth couples)

Third Figure Leads Promenade around each other and pass to the couple on the right! Cross right hands, change partners, and pass to the gentlemen's place! Leads polka! (Sides repeat the same)

Fourth Figure First and third couples right and left! First polka! Leads polka! All polka! (Third and second couples, second and fourth, fourth and first, repeat the change)

Fifth Figure All Forward and Back! Ladies one place to the right! Ladies Double Chain! Turn corners! All polka! (Repeat until all are back to places) All polka to seats!

POLKA QUADRILLE

Preliminary Call (See "The Beginner's Set")

Figure

Take that gentleman and half Promenade! Ladies Half Chain! Take your partner and Half Promenade to place! Grand Chain all the way around! Four ladies to the center!

Gents circle on the outside! Form a basket and circle eight as you are! Reverse positions with gents in the center, and circle eight the other way around!

Final Call (See "The Beginner's Set")

Dance continues until all couples have performed the figure.

THE PAUL JONES

Form with any number of couples.

Music: Two-four and three-four time.

Honor your partner and lady on the left! All join hands and circle to the left!

Balance All!

Swing your partners! Left Alamand! Once and a Half and Right and Left Grand!

Meet your partners and waltz! Ladies step forward and the gents step back! Change partners and waltz!

Meet your partners and all Promenade!

Waltz Quadrille

(De Gormo)

Music: Combination of Galop and Waltz.

Preliminary Call (See "The Beginner's Set")

First Figure First four Right and Left! Balance four and turn! Ladies chain! All waltz!

Second Figure First two forward and back! Cross over! First four forward and back! Turn to places! All waltz! (Repeat three times)

Third Figure First four cross over with right hand! Back with left! Balance in a square! Turn to place! All waltz! (Repeat)

Fourth Figure Four ladies forward and salute! Four gents the same! All chasse and turn corners with right hand! (Slow time) Turn partners with left hand! Grand Right and Left half around! (Quick time) On to place! All galop around the hall to seats!

American National Lancers

(The Saratoga)

Preliminary Call (See "The Beginner's Set")

First Figure First four forward and back with right hand couples! Turn opposite with both hands and return to place!

First four join hands and pass between sides! Return outside, sides between, hands joined! Address corners! Turn corners! Sides repeat to right!

Second Figure First four forward and back with right hand couples! Leave ladies in center facing partners! Address!

All forward and back! Turn partners to place! Promenade, arm in arm, around the opposite couple! Sides repeat to right!

Third Figure First four forward and back with the right hand couple! Forward again! Address and return to place! Ladies' Chain with the same couple! Sides repeat to the right!

Fourth Figure First four lead to the right! Address! Exchange ladies, lead to the opposite! Address! Exchange ladies, lead to place!

Address center! Right and left with right-hand couples! Sides repeat, leaving all in original places!

Fifth Figure Grand Right and Left half way around! Pass partner, turn and address! Reverse Grand Right and Left back! Address partner in place! First couple Promenade around inside of set, face outward! Third and fourth couple fall in line! All forward and back! Separate, forming two lines, facing partners! Head couple join hands, down the center and back! All forward and back in two lines, turn partners to place!

Final Call (See "The Beginner's Set")

THE LANCERS

Preliminary Call (See "The Beginner's Set")

First Figure First four forward and back! Turn opposite once around and return to place! First couple join hands and pass between second couple!

Second couple join hands and pass between first! Address corner! Turn corner! Sides repeat!

Second Figure First four forward and back! Forward and leave ladies in the center facing partners! Address partners! Forward and back, passing partner on the left!

Turn partners! Side four separate, join hands with first four! Forward and back in two lines! Forward, turn partners to place! Sides' repeat!

Third Figure First four forward and back! Forward! Address partners and return to place! Ladies chain! Sides repeat!

Fourth Figure First four lead to the right! Address! Promenade half way! Address to place!

Address opposite couple! Right and Left Four! Sides repeat! (Then to the left).

218

Fifth Figure Address Partners! Grand Right and Left! Address partners at meeting! First couple Promenade around inside· of the set facing out! Third and fourth couple fall in line!

Left and Right Glide! March! Ladies to the Right and gents to the left! Join hands and forward and back in two lines! Forward and turn partners to place!

Final Call (See "The Beginner's Set")

THE COTILLION

(Tune "The Cotillion" on page 140)

Form a set with eight or more couples. Place chairs around the room in a semi-circle. Each couple should tie their chairs together with a pocket-handkerchief or ribbon. A leader is chosen who arranges the figures to be used. No lady or gentleman may refuse to dance.

Music: Waltz, Redowa, Polka and Galop or Mazurka.

The leader may start and stop the music at will with a castinet and let the orchestra know what to play next.

Each number is commenced by the leader and partner, or by all waltzing around the inside of the charmed circle.

I

Lawn Tennis

The leader selects five ladies. Leader's partner selects six gents. Leader and his partner hold up sheet for net. All the ladies on one side of the sheet, gents on the other side. Ladies bat a ball over the sheet in rotation.

The gentleman catching the ball will step around the net, take the lady who served the ball for his partner and promenade or waltz until all the ladies have partners. Lone gent takes his seat. Leader waltzes with partner.

II

The Pyramid

Ladies form pyramid. Equal number of gentlemen join hands in a line and wind around first lady, then around next two, next three, and so on. Then reverse the movement until conductor arrives in front of first lady, with whom he waltzes. Other gents waltz with the nearest ladies.

Rearrange the pyramid as often as desired.

III

The Grand Round

Any number, four or more, lead off. Each gentleman selects another gentleman, each lady selects another lady. The ladies join hands in a circle. Gents form a circle around ladies' circle. All circle to the left one complete circle, then break. First gent takes his partner directly through circle.

Second gent with second lady follow, then third gent and lady, and so on. Gents go to the right and ladies to the left. They remain in two curved lines, gents in one, ladies in the other. Leader waltzes with partner down the center. Each couple follow successively and quickly until all waltz.

IV

The Zigzags

Any number of couples, six or more, place themselves in line all facing in the same direction. They keep close to partners, each couple about three feet apart.

The rear couple commence waltzing zigzag through the column, each couple following in rotation until all are waltzing. Continue waltzing until signaled to seats.

V

The Magic Hat

First couple lead off. The leader gives his lady a hat, which she presents to several other ladies who deposit in it some article, such as a glove, a key, handkerchief, etc.

She then presents the hat to the gentlemen, who each take one of the articles and dance with the lady to whom it belongs.

Repeat as desired.

VI

The Serpent

First couple lead off. The gentleman leaves his lady in a corner of the room facing the wall. Then he brings forward four or five more ladies and places them in a line behind his partner singly, leaving about two feet space between each one.

He then selects as many gentlemen (including himself) as there are ladies, with whom he forms a loose chain and conducts them rapidly in a course between the ladies (commencing with the last lady) until he reaches his partner. He then claps his hands and each gentleman dances with the lady nearest him.

THE SPANISH WALTZ

Form a set of any number of couples, in sets of two couples facing each other.

First Part Lady and gent of each couple advance separately to their vis-a-vis. Retire, and waltz separately to opposite sides. Then waltz back to place with partner. Repeat this movement again.

Second Part All join hands in a circle. Forward and back, the gentleman turning the lady on his left, hand over head, into his place while he steps into hers. Repeat this four times, when the original place will be reached.

Third Part Couples waltz twice around their own sets and pass on to meet the next couples. Repeat the figure with them and continue until original *vis-a-vis* is met.

REELS

The Virginia

Form a set with six couples, gents opposite ladies.

Preliminary Call (See "The Beginner's Set")

Figure

First lady and foot gent meet in the center! Balance and return to places! First gent and foot lady same! First lady and foot gent meet and swing with left hand! First gent and foot lady same! First lady and foot gent meet and swing with right hand! First gent and foot lady same! First couple give right hands and swing Once and a Half! Swing second with the right hand!

Partner with the left! Third with the right! Partner with the left! Fourth with the right! Partner with the left! Fifth with the right! Partner with the left! Sixth with the right! Partner with the left! Up the center with partner and swing! All lead around! Ladies to the right and gents to the left! First couple down the center to the foot and stop! Next lady and foot gent meet in center!

Dance continues until all have performed the figure.

Final Call (See "The Beginner's Set")

THE MOUNTAIN

Form a set of six people. A lady between two gents faces similar three opposite. Same up and down the hall.

Figure

All forward and back! Each lady execute the reel with her right-hand partner! Then with her left-hand partner back to place!

Three hands around and back again! All forward and back! Forward again and pass through opposite! Face the next three

Dance continues until all have performed the figure.

SIX-HAND

Form a set with six couples.

Preliminary Call (See "The Beginner's Set")

Figures

First couple cross over! Go outside of second couple! Inside between second and third! Pass outside of third couple up to the head and back to place!

As first gent passes outside of second lady, she turns and follows. As he passes inside and around below third lady, she follows. Thus the second and third ladies make a straight right and left with each other.

The gent now makes the same changes with the second and third gents, and the first lady at the same time with the second and third ladies.

First couple down the center and back! Down the center and cast off right and left! Next couple cross over!

Final Call (See "The Beginner's Set")

Dance continues until all have performed the figure.

DESCRIPTION OF ROUND DANCES

DESCRIPTION OF ROUND DANCES

ROUND DANCE INSTRUCTIONS

The Five Positions

1st. Stand with weight of body equally on both feet with heels together, toes turned out.

2nd. Glide right foot directly to right, bending left knee.

3rd. Place right heel in hollow of left foot.

4th. Glide right foot forward from 1st or 3rd position.

5th. Place right heel at side of toe of left foot.

Above positions also to be taken with left foot.

In movements where foot is raised, keep toe well pointed toward floor.

THE SCHOTTISCHE

The schottische consists of two parts. Each differs in character and occupies together four bars of music.

The first part consists of eight steps — or rather six steps and two hops. The second part is a rotary movement, accomplished by four hops on alternate feet, counting "One and two, three and four." The second and fifth waltz steps are taken lightly and rapidly at the word "and."

The Steps

FIRST PART

First Step Bend both knees slightly. Slide the left to second position, resting the weight of the body thereon.

Second Step With a light spring on the left foot bring the right foot to the place of the left. In so doing point the left foot in the second position, slightly raised.

Third Step Transfer the whole weight of the body to the left leg while bending the knee. At the same time raise the right foot behind to third position, with the toes pointed downwards.

Fourth Step Hop very slightly on the left foot. Repeat the movement with the right foot. Finish with the weight of the body on the right leg. This completes two bars and should be counted: "One, two, three, hop. One, two, three, hop."

SECOND PART

First Step Transfer the whole weight of the body to the left leg while bending the knee. At the same time raise the right foot behind, third position, with toe pointed downwards.

Second Step Hop very slightly on left foot, and in so doing turn half round.

Third Step Right foot down.

Fourth Step Hop, turning half round. Repeat the above four steps. The second part is generally waltzed, and is accomplished as explained in the counting.

THE MILITARY SCHOTTISCHE

Partners stand side by side for the first part, (four bars). The lady's left hand rests in the right hand of her partner.

In the second part, (four bars) partners dance together as in an ordinary round dance.

The Steps

FIRST PART

First Step Slide the left foot to fourth position.

Second Step With a light spring on the left foot, bring the right foot to place of the left. In so doing point the left foot, slightly raised in front, in the fourth position.

Third Step Spring forward on the left foot, raising the right behind.

Fourth Step Make a slight hop on the left foot. Extend the right in front with toe pointed downwards. Repeat the movement, commencing with the right foot, (the foot the lady begins with). The two movements are again repeated to complete the first four bars.

SECOND PART

Hold as in an ordinary round dance. Waltz four bars as explained in the schottische.

THE YORKE

The Yorke is a derivation of the Polka. It introduces a mazurka movement, at pleasure, by the lady with her right foot and the gentleman with his left. It requires four bars of music for each revolution. Half turns are made at the second bar and each alternate bar thereafter.

Lady slides right foot to 2nd position counting "one." Slides left foot to 1st position, counting "two." Then slides right foot again to second position and raises right foot from floor, toe pointed, counting "and three."

Then hop lightly on left foot and place weight on right foot. Slide right foot sideways and forward about six inches (hop-slide), counting "one." Draw left to right foot in first position, counting "two." Leap from left to right foot, counting "three." Slide the left foot to 1st position, counting "one." Repeat these steps with opposite foot, making the leap backwards as in the waltz.

To give the mazurka effect, one can strike the heels together.

To be graceful in this dance, special attention must be paid to the hop-slide.

The Polka Mazurka

The Polka-Mazurka is in three-four time, and consists of six steps, on the last of which a half turn is made.

Position: Third.

First Step First step of the Polka.

Second Step Second step of the Polka.

Third Step Slide the left foot back to the side of the right leg, the toe being pointed downwards and off the floor, then hop on the right foot.

Fourth, Fifth and Sixth Steps Polka half round. The first three steps should be taken sideways, partners facing each other.

The Redowa

The Redowa is in three-four time. The original style of this dance is almost lost. It began with a promenade movement, later changed to a circular figure. Then a kind of elongated polka step was substituted for the other movements.

Position: Third.

The Steps

First Step Spring on the right foot into the 2nd position, turning half round and well bending the knee, the right foot meanwhile being drawn up close in front over the instep of the left. Then slide right foot to 2nd position.

Second Step Transfer the weight of the body to the right foot.

Third Step Draw up left foot into 5th position and rest the weight on it, raising the right foot slightly in front.

Fourth Step Spring on the right foot in fourth position with bended knee. Then turn half round, at the same time bringing the left foot close up behind the right, and slide the left foot into second position.

Fifth Step Transfer the whole weight of the body to the left foot.

Sixth Step Draw up the right foot into the fifth position, and rest the weight thereon.

The Polka

The Polka consists of three steps and one movement, or rise. A momentary pause may be substituted for this rise. But it must be understood that the preliminary rise before the first step gives all the necessary lightness and grace that is requisite for the proper performance of this dance.

The Steps

First Step Rise on the sole of the right foot, having the left foot raised behind and slightly pointed downwards without touching the floor.

Drop down on the right foot and at the same time glide the left foot to second position, transferring the weight of the body thereon.

Second Step With a light spring on the left foot, bring the right foot quickly down to the place which the left foot occupied, at the same time raising the left.

Third Step Spring on to the left foot. At the same time turn half round and draw the right foot up behind, slightly pointed downwards.

Repeat above three steps to complete circle, but start with right foot.

These steps may be taken forward or backward and to right or left, by a slight alteration of the first step.

All the steps should be made with elasticity, the knees slightly bent, and entirely on the toes.

HEEL AND TOE POLKA

Both lady and gentleman hop on right foot and place left foot to the side in second position, with heel upon the floor, toe up, counting "one." Hop on right foot and at the same time place left foot in fifth position, toe on floor, heel raised, counting "two." Turn half round, then repeat the first two steps with opposite foot. Turn half round to the original position.

This dance may be continued as a plain polka.

THE GALOP

In the Galop the music is in two-four time and, as a rule, played quickly.

There are two kinds of steps used: one for going forward and the other for turning round.

The forward movement is a perfectly natural one and will be easily understood. The turning movement is accomplished by using the ordinary waltz step, counting "one and two, one and two," letting the fifth steps come in at the word "and."

The Steps

Position Right foot in front.
First Step Slide the left foot to second position with a gentle spring on the right foot.

Second Step Bring the right foot up to the left, with a light spring on the left foot.

Repeat, alternating right and left foot in front.

THE MINUET

Position Stand beside partner, march style, gentleman on the right and lady on the left. Join hands, shoulder high. Steps to be taken a la Minuet.

FIRST PART

Music: In three-four time, twenty-four measures per minute.

Steps Left foot forward to fourth position (one). Right foot forward to fourth position (two). Left foot forward to fourth position (three). Extend right foot forward to fourth position, touching the toe to the floor (four). Pose in that position (five and six). Turn half round towards partner, face opposite direction, change hands, step right foot forward to fourth position (one).

Step left foot forward to fourth position (two). Right foot forward to fourth position (three). Left foot forward to fourth position (four). Pose in that position (five and six). Face partner, left foot to second position (one). Bring right foot back to fifth position (two). Left foot to second position (three). Right foot forward to fourth position, partly crossed, joined hands raised (four). Pose in that position (five and six). Right foot to second position (one). Swing left foot around right foot and pirouette, disengage hands (two and three). Bow and take position first described (four, five and six).

SECOND PART

Position: Same as first. Steps to be taken a la Polka.
Music: In two-four time, fifty-five measures per minute.

Steps Left foot forward to fourth position (one). **Right foot** to fifth position and back. Left foot forward to fourth position (two). Swing right foot forward to fourth position, touch toe lightly (one). Swing the same foot around, turning one-half, toward partner, face opposite direction, change hands and touch the toe lightly, fourth position forward (two). Right foot forward to fourth position (one). Swing the same foot, face partner and take waltz position, to second position (two). Then dance the plain polka four measures.

Repeat the whole second part, making sixteen measures of polka music.

The forward movements in the second part are to be taken in a running manner.

THE VARSOVIENNE

The varsovienne is a very simple dance. The first step is same as the polka with the knee well bent on the third movement, turning half round, the opposite foot being slightly raised behind in the fifth position. This occupies one bar of music. At four (the commencement of the second bar), the bent knee is gradually straightened without any jerk, and the other foot at the same time is slid into second position, the toe being extensively pointed, and the body inclining toward it till the remainder of the bar is finished.

The step is again performed with the right foot and continued alternately for sixteen bars, each step requiring two bars for completion.

The first movement is repeated eight times. The second step consists of the first part of the polka, done twice, occupying two bars of music. This is followed by one step of the first movement, requiring two more bars. This step, as well as the third, requiring four bars, is only performed four times. The first movement being repeated after each of them.

The third part, consists of the first step danced three times before pointing the foot in second position, pausing; or in other words, it is the polka movement danced with a bent knee three times successively before pointing the opposite foot.

OLD TIME PLAY PARTY

Songs

With Dancing Games

JIM-ALONG JOSEY

(The chorus of above play-party song is the same as
fiddle tune "Run, Nigger, Run." See page 37)

One foot up
    And one foot down.
Honor your partners
    And swing 'em all around.

Cornstalk fiddle
    And a shoe-string bow.
If this ain't dancing
    I don't know.

Met Miss Sally
    Down the street.
I'm here to tell you
    She looked sweet.

Sam King's buggy
    It broke down,
And Mary Ann
    Had to walk to town.

I made a cake.
    Well, I do declare!
It took first prize
    At the County Fair.

Had a piece-a cake
    And had a piece-a pie.
We'll all say good-night,
    But we won't say good-bye.

Chorus

Hey, Jim along,
    And a-Jim along a-Josey!
Hey, Jim along,
    And a-Jim along a-Joe!

239

All players join hands and circle to the left. Balance all. Swing partners. Alamande left and Right and Left Grand. Promenade. First couple balance to the couple on the right. Four hands around. Ladies do, gents you know. Balance to the next couple. Repeat "four hands around, ladies do, gents, you know," with three remaining couples. Then balance home and Right and Left Grand. Continue until all couples have been around. (Final Grand Right and Left may be extended by using the Once and a Half and Right and Left on. Or, Once and a Half and Right and Left back, to the Promenade).

SKIP-TO-MY-LOU

Look at the greenie, standing there,
　　Look at the greenie, standing there,
Look at the greenie, standing there,
　　Skip-to-my-lou, my darling.

I lost my pardner, skip-to-my-lou,
　　I lost my pardner, skip-to-my-lou,
I lost my pardner, skip-to-my-lou,
　　Skip-to-my-lou, my darling.

I'll get another one, sweeter, too,

    I'll get another one, sweeter, too,

I'll get another one, sweeter, too,

    Skip-to-my-lou, my darling.

Join hands and circle with odd lady or gent, (the greenie) inside the ring. Balance and swing partners. Then Grand Right and Left, in which the odd lady or gent joins the chain. When around to original position someone is always left without a partner, whereupon this one becomes the greenie.

MAKE A CAKE FOR CHARLEY

Oh, Charley, he is a fine young man,

    Oh, Charley, he's a dandy.

Oh, Charley, he can kiss the girls,

    As sweet as sugar candy.

Oh, I won't have none of your weevily wheat,

    And I won't have none of your barley.

I'll take the very best of wheat

    To make a cake for Charley.

Oh, Charley, he is a fine young man,

Oh, Charley, he's a dandy.

Oh, Charley, he can kiss the girls,

As sweet as sugar candy.

The higher up in the cherry tree,

The riper grows the berry.

The more you hug and kiss the girls

The sooner they will marry.

Form with four couples and one odd gent, (Charley). Join hands and circle to the left with Charley in the center. First lady swings first gent, then swings Charley down the center and casts off, lady to the right and gent to the left, and the first gent becomes Charley.

Next lady swings her partner and Charley, executing same figure as first couple, until each couple have been around the set. Final Grand Right and Left and Promenade, in which one gent is left without a partner. He then becomes Charley for the evening, choosing and directing other dances and games of the party.

DOWN THE OHIO

(The first eight bars of "Down The Ohio" are the same as fiddle tune "Captain." See page 120)

The steamer is coming round the bend,

    Oh, Dinah, go kill the old fat hen.

You'll have to feed some hungry men,

    As the Captain shouts: "Heave Ho!"

The whistle is blowing for Hollenbeck,

    The darkies are dancing on the deck.

You can hear them singing "Old Dan Peck."

    As the Captain shouts: "Heave Ho!"

Chorus

Down the river, oh, down the river,

    Oh, down the river we go!

Down the river, oh, down the river,

    Oh, down the Ohio!

Swing partners and form a reel. Ladies to the center with left hands across. Link right arms with partners and turn to the right. Break and swing. Reverse, with gents to the center and turn to the left. Break and swing partners. Alamande Left. Grand Right and Left and Promenade. Then three remaining couples perform same figure. The chorus is repeated in the Grand Right and Left and to make up for any added changes in the figure.

SHOOT THE BUFFALO

We'll load the covered wagons
    And we'll hit the Indian trail.
We'll camp along the rivers,
    When the moon shines pale.
We'll dance around the camp fire,
    Where the shadows come and go,
And when our Indian guide comes along,
    We'll hunt the buffalo.

Chief Oronoco's daughter,
    One we'll honor with great pride.
I'll forfeit forty ponies
    If she'll be my bride.
And if she dare to spurn us
    We will take our goods and go,

Till another Indian maid comes along,

    We'll hunt the buffalo.

Chorus

We'll shoot the buffalo,

    We'll shoot the buffalo.

We'll rally round the cane-brake

    And shoot the buffalo.

Form with four or more couples. Ladies join hands and circle left, with gents inside the ring facing outward. Coming to the place in the verse "And when our Indian guide comes along," each lady, at the words "comes along," swings the gent facing her to place.

Beginning with the chorus, all balance and swing again. Alamande Left. Grand Right and Left and Promenade. The chorus is repeated as often as necessary for the Grand Right and Left, depending on the number of couples in the set. Second time: Gents join hands and circle with ladies inside the ring.

I SENT MY BROWN JUG DOWN TO TOWN

I sent my brown jug down to town,

    I sent my brown jug down to town.

It came back full of bounce around,

    Sing fol-de-rol-de-ray.

The preacher came to save a sinner,
    The preacher came to save a sinner.
Now we'll all have chicken pie for dinner,
    Sing fol-de-rol-de-ray.

I ran away to the old race track,
    Lost my money, I'm afraid to go back.
Dad's laying awake with the old boot-jack,
    Sing fol-de-rol-de-ray.

Going to dance my way up the golden stair,
    If old Mr. Satan don't get me by the hair,
I'll see you all when you get there.
    Sing fol-de-rol-de-ray.

First gent swings first lady and sends her around the set to swing each gent. When she returns to her partner all balance and swing. Alemande Left. Right and Left Grand and Promenade.

The first verse is sung as each couple goes through the figure. Other verses are used in the Grand Right and Left.

WE'LL ALL GO DOWN TO ROUSERS

(The first eight bars of "We'll All Go Down to Rousers" are the same as "We Won't Go Home Till Morning." See page 97)

We'll all go down to Rousers,
    We'll all go down to Rousers,
We'll all go down to Rousers,
    To get some lager beer.

They put the pig in the parlor,
    They put the pig in the parlor,
They put the pig in the parlor,
    And that was Irish too.

Johnny fell out of the haymow,
    Johnny fell out of the haymow,
Johnny fell out of the haymow,
    And that was Irish too.

We'll all go down to Rousers,
    We'll all go down to Rousers,
We'll all go down to Rousers,
    To get some lager beer.

Chorus
Then honor to the ladies,
And swing them round the waist.
Then right and left through till
    you meet your pardner,
And promenade back to your place.

247

All join hands and circle left. (Eight bars, which is a verse).
The words of the chorus indicate all the changes of the set, the
chorus being used after each verse.

OLD BRASS WAGON

(Music of above play-party song is a variation of
fiddle tune "Drunken Sailor." See page 74)

All join hands, Old Brass Wagon.
  Circle to the left, Old Brass Wagon.
Circle to the left, Old Brass Wagon.
  You're the one, my darling.

Swing your partners, Old Brass Wagon.
  Alamande left, Old Brass Wagon.
Grand Right and Left, Old Brass Wagon.
  You're the one, my darling.

Grand Right and Left, Old Brass Wagon.
  Promenade home, Old Brass Wagon.
Promenade home, Old Brass Wagon.
  You're the one, my darling.

Polka up and down, Old Brass Wagon.

Polka up and down, Old Brass Wagon.

Polka up and down, Old Brass Wagon.

You're the one, my darling.

All the changes for this old play-party dance are indicated in its verses. However, it was sometimes made to fit more intricate dance calls.

(See also "Old John Brown Had a Little Indian." on page 448)

CHILDREN'S PLAY SONGS

OF THE

VILLAGE GREEN

OLD JUBITER

(Fiddle tune on page 99)

The story Old Jubiter
Told you and me,
The night we sat under
The juniper tree.

At the end of the rainbow
Is what we were told,
We'll each find a treasure
Of bright shiny gold.

Chorus
Of bright shiny gold,
Of bright shiny gold.
Oh, where is the treasure
Of bright shiny gold?

First a leader is chosen. Then all join hands and circle. Release hands and follow the leader, single file, breaking out and away from the circle forming a rainbow, players spacing out about three feet apart. About face. The leader starts weaving right and left through, and all in turn follow to take their places at the rainbow's end.

THE MILLER BOY

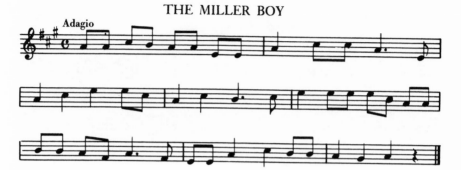

Happy is the miller boy that lives by the mill,

The wheel goes round with a free goodwill.

One hand in the hopper and the other in the sack,

The ladies step forward and the gents step back.

Form a wheel. Girls move to center. Join right hands with opposite girls. Link arms with partners and turn the wheel. Girl drops partner at last line of verse. Picks up partner ahead and wheel is continued until all come to original partners. Boys move to center. Reverse wheel and follow same procedure as for girls.

RING-A-ROUND OF ROSES

Ring-a-round of roses,

A pocket full of posies.

A bow here and a bow there,

A bow to the center.

Ring-a-round of roses,

A pocket full of posies.

At-choo! At-choo!

And blow them all down.

All join hands and circle. Bow to the right and to the left, then
to the center. At "At-choo!" all fall down.

PRINCE WILLIAM

Prince William was King James's son,

And in the royal race he won.

He wore a star upon his breast,

Pointing to the East and West.

Go to the East, go to the West,

Go choose the one that you love best.

If he's not here to take your part,

Choose another with all your heart.

255

Down on this carpet you must kneel,

As sure as the grass grows in the field.

You choose her bright, now kiss her sweet,

Then you may rise upon your feet.

All join hands and circle with one girl or boy in the center. The one in the center goes to the East and then to the West and chooses a partner. Repeat.

GREEN GRAVEL

Green gravel! Green gravel!

The grass is so green,

But nowhere my lover

Is here to be seen.

Green gravel! Green gravel!

Your true love is dead.

He sent you a letter

To turn back your head.

Green gravel! Green gravel!

Go kneel by his side.

One touch of your hands

And he'll come back to life.

Form a ring with one girl in the center. Join hands and circle. The girl in the center points, in time to the rhythm of the song, to each girl in rotation until one is chosen who, at the words "To turn back your head," faces outward. (Keep the circle moving).

The first verse is now repeated while a boy is chosen and blindfolded, who lies down in the center of the ring. The girl facing outward now turns again facing the center, and a different girl is pointed out who slips in and kneels beside the boy. (The object is to confuse the boy as to which girl is there). Also, she may grab him at any word in the verse, whereas he will be expecting her to touch him at the words "One touch of your hands." (He may remove the blindfold here, but not before).

The first verse is repeated as often as necessary, depending on the number of players and the time required to arrange the play.

ROUND THE MULBERRY BUSH

Here we go round the mulberry bush,

The mulberry bush, the mulberry bush.

Here we go round the mulberry bush,

So early in the morning.

This is the way we wash our clothes,

Wash our clothes, wash our clothes.

This is the way we wash our clothes,
    So early Monday morning.

This is the way we iron our clothes,
    Iron our clothes, iron our clothes.
This is the way we iron our clothes,
    So early Tuesday morning.

This is the way we scrub the floor,
    Scrub the floor, scrub the floor.
This is the way we scrub the floor,
    So early Wednesday morning.

This is the way we mend our clothes,
    Mend our clothes, mend our clothes.
This is the way we mend our clothes,
    So early Thursday morning.

This is the way we sweep the house,
    Sweep the house, sweep the house.
This is the way we sweep the house,
    So early Friday morning.

This is the way we bake our bread,
    Bake our bread, bake our bread.
This is the way we bake our bread,
    So early Saturday morning.

This is the way we go to church,

Go to church, go to church.

This is the way we go to church,

So early Sunday morning.

All join hands and circle. Stop and go through motions to indicate ironing clothes, etc.

YANKEE DOODLE

Yankee Doodle went to town,

Riding on a pony.

He stuck a feather in his cap

And called it Macaroni.

Yankee Doodle went to town,

To take a load of switches.

He wore his mother's canton gown,

And his daddy's leather britches.

259

Chorus

Yankee Doodle is a dude,

Yankee Doodle dandy.

Yankee Doodle swing the girls,

As sweet as sugar candy.

Go single file in circle to left. Boys turn, facing the girls at beginning of the chorus. Swing right and left around to partners and promenade.

(Other verses on page 396)

SALLY GO ROUND THE CHIMNEY POT

Sally go round the stars,

Sally go round the moon.

Sally go round the chimney-pot

On a Sunday afternoon. Who-eee!

Join hands and skip in a circle to the right. At the end of verse all shout "who-eee!" All kick forward with right foot and then circle left. Kick with left foot and circle right. Repeat.

GO IN AND OUT THE WINDOW

Go round and round the valley,
Go round and round the valley,
Go round and round the valley,
As we have done before.

Go forth and choose your lover,
Go forth and choose your lover,
Go forth and choose your lover,
As we have done before.

Go in and out the window,
Go in and out the window,
Go in and out the window,
As we have done before.

Join hands and circle with one player in the center. Stop at end of first verse while player in center chooses partner. The circle spreads out with clasped hands raised, while the two players weave in and out of arches. After going through the last arch the two players remain on outside of the circle.

All circle again with two outside going around in the opposite direction. Stop till the next odd player inside the circle has chosen partner. Then the four go "In and out the windows" until all have gone through the arch made by the last remaining two players. All join hands except odd player left over, who remains inside the circle for the next game.

LONDON BRIDGE IS FALLING DOWN

London bridge is falling down,
    Falling down, falling down.
London bridge is falling down,
    My fair lady.

Build it up with iron bars,
    Iron bars, iron bars.
Build it up with iron bars,
    My fair lady.

Iron bars will bend and break,
    Bend and break, bend and break.
Iron bars will bend and break,
    My fair lady.

Build it up with gold and silver,
    Gold and silver, gold and silver.
Gold and silver will be stolen away,
    My fair lady.

Get a man to watch all night,
    Watch all night, watch all night.
Suppose the man should fall asleep,
    My fair lady.

Get a dog to bark all night,
   Bark all night, bark all night.
Suppose the dog should find a bone,
   My fair lady.

Here's a prisoner I have got,
   I have got, I have got.
Here's a prisoner I have got,
   My fair lady.

What's the prisoner done to you?
   Done to you, done to you?
Stole my hat and lost my keys,
   My fair lady.

Off to prison he must go,
   He must go, he must go.
Off to prison he must go,
   My fair lady.

Two of the players join hands and hold them high, forming the bridge for the others to pass under. The other players form a line single file, placing hands on shoulders while passing under the arch, as the verses are sung alternately by the players passing under and the two forming the arch.

As the words "Here's a prisoner I have got" are sung, the one who is passing under is caught by the falling bridge, as the ones forming the arch drop their arms. The prisoner is then taken off to one side and asked to choose between two objects there, which represent the two sides of the bridge. One might be a bicycle, the other a pony. The prisoner lines up at back of the side he has chosen. When all prisoners have been assigned, all clasp arms around the one in front and pull tug-of-war.

HIP-ETTY-HOP

Hip-etty-hop to the barber shop,

To get a stick of candy.

One for you and one for me,

And one for sister Mandy.

This little song sketch has been used by the children of several generations. It was a usual habit for two children walking along together to school, or on other occasions, to place their arms about each other's waists and skip along to the song of "Hip-etty-hop."

THE FARMER IN THE DELL

The farmer in the dell
    The farmer in the dell.
Heigh-o! the ferry-o!
    The farmer in the dell.

The farmer takes a wife,
    The farmer takes a wife.
Heigh-o! the ferry-o!
    The farmer takes a wife.

The wife takes a child,
    The wife takes a child.
Heigh-o! the ferry-o!
    The wife takes a child.

The child takes a nurse.
    The child takes a nurse.
Heigh-o! the ferry-o!
    The child takes a nurse.

The nurse takes a dog,
    The nurse takes a dog.
Heigh-o! the ferry-o!
    The nurse takes a dog.

The dog takes a cat,
    The dog takes a cat.

Heigh-o! the ferry-o!
    The dog takes a cat.

The cat takes a rat,
    The cat takes a rat.
Heigh-o! the ferry-o!
    The cat takes a rat.

The rat takes the cheese,
    The rat takes the cheese.
Heigh-o! the ferry-o!
    The rat takes the cheese.

The cheese stands alone,
    The cheese stands alone.
Heigh-o! the ferry-o!
    The farmer in the dell.

Join hands and circle with one odd player in center. Beginning with the second verse, the farmer in the center chooses one from the circle for his wife; the wife chooses one for the child; the child chooses nurse, etc., as the verses indicate, until the "cheese" stands alone. All return to the circle except the cheese, who is the farmer in the next game.

OLD-TIME BALLADS

AND

SONGS OF ENTERTAINMENT

SILVER BELLS OF MEMORY

In the hush of eventide,
    Sitting by my cottage door,
Mem'ries softly seem to glide,
    Backward to the days of yore.

And I hear in tuneful swells,
    Sweetest notes of melody,
'Tis the sound of silver bells,
    Silver bells of memory.

Many faces have grown old,
    Many forms been laid to rest,
Underneath the churchyard mold,
    Ones I love the most and best.

And I hear in changeful swells,

   Floating on the breeze to me,

Low_and soft as silver bells,

   Now, the bells of memory.

Chorus

Silver bells! Silver bells!

   Silver bells of memory.

Silver bells! Silver bells!

   Silver bells of memory.

MY BOYHOOD HAPPY DAYS DOWN ON THE FARM

Refrain

D.S. ℀

When a boy I used to dwell,

In a home I loved so well,

Far away among the clover and the bees.

Where the morning glory vine,

Round the cabin porch did twine,

And the robin redbreast sang among the trees.

There were brothers young and gay,
    And a father old and gray,
And a mother dear to shield us from all harm.
    There I spent life's sunny hours,
Running wild among the flowers,
    In my boyhood happy days down on the farm.

Refrain

Many weary years have passed
    Since I saw the old home last,
And the mem'ry dear, steals o'er me like a charm.
    Every old familiar place,
Every kind and loving face,
    In my boyhood happy home down on the farm.

And today as I drew near,
    That old place I love so dear,
A stranger came to meet me at the door.
    Round the place there's many a change,
And the faces all seem strange,
    Not a loved one comes to meet me as of yore.

For my mother dear, is laid
    'Neath the elm tree's quiet shade,
Where the golden Summer sun shines bright and warm.
    Over near the old fireplace,
There I see a stranger's face
    In my father's old arm-chair down on the farm.

JOSHUA EBENEZER FRY

I'm the Constable of Pumpkinville,
    Jist traded hosses at the mill.
My name's Joshua
    Ebenezer Fry.

I know a thing or two,
    Yew bet yer life I do.
Yew cain't fool me
    'Cause I'm too dern'd sly.

Wal, I swan!

    I must be gittin' on.

Giddap, Napoleon!

    It looks like rain.

I'll shoot a hawk!

    If the critter didn't balk,

I'll lick Jed Hawkins,

    Sure as Joshua's my name.

I went to the County Fair,

    Met a city slicker there.

He says: "Gimme two tens

    Fer a five."

I says: "Ye derned fool,

    I be the Constabule.

Now you're arrested

    Jist as sure as you're alive."

Chorus

Wal, I swan!

    I must be gittin' on.

Giddap, Napoleon!

    It looks like rain.

I'll bet two bits

    The money's counterfeit,

That city feller gimme

    Comin' down on the train.

I hitched up the old mare,
    Druv 'er to the County Fair.
Took first prize,
    On a load of squash.
I got so derned full,
    I went and sold the red bull,
And give away the cow
    That wore the silver bell.

Chorus

Wal, I swan!
    I must be gittin' on.
Giddap, Napoleon!
    It looks like rain.
I'll be derned!
    If the butter ain't churned.
Now we'll have some buttermilk,
    Or Josh is not my name.

I got home so derned late,
    Couldn't find the barn gate.
Ma says: "Joshua!
    Is it possible?
Yew air a disgrace.
    Yew ort to go and hide yer face.
I never seed sich actions
    Fer to be a Constibule."

275

Chorus

Wal, I swan!

I must be gittin' on.

Giddap, Napoleon!

It looks like rain.

I'll be switched,

And the hay ain't pitched.

Drap in when yew're

Over to the farm again.

SHE'LL BE COMIN' ROUND THE MOUNTAIN

She'll be comin' round the mountain when she comes,

She'll be comin' round the mountain when she comes,

She'll be comin' round the mountain,

She'll be comin' round the mountain,

She'll be comin' round the mountain when she comes.

She'll be drivin' six white horses when she comes,
She'll be drivin' six white horses when she comes,
She'll be drivin' six white horses,
She'll be drivin' six white horses,
She'll be drivin' six white horses when she comes.

Oh, we'll all go out to meet her when she comes,
Oh, we'll all go out to meet her when she comes,
We'll kill the old red rooster,
We'll kill the old red rooster,
And we'll all have chicken and dumplins' when she comes.

BRIDGET DONOHUE

Oh, Bridget Donohue, I dearly do love you,
Altho' I'm in America, to you I will be true.
I sent my love a picture, I did upon my word,
'Twas not the picture of myself, but the picture of a bird.
" 'Tis the American Eagle," says I, "Miss Donohue,
There's room beneath this eagle's wings to shelter you and me.
Oh, Bridget Donohue, I'll tell you what I'll do,
You take the name of Patterson and I'll take Donohue."

HISTORY OF THE WORLD

(See also "Uncle Sam's Farm" on page 446)

Oh, I come from ol' Virginny,
With my head full of knowledge,
And I never went to free school,
Nor airy other college.
But one thing I will tell you,
Which is a solemn fact.
I'll tell you how this world was made,
In the twinkling of a crack.

Oh, this world was made in six days,
    And then they made the sky,
And then they hung it overhead,
    And left it there to dry.
And then they made the stars,
    Out of pretty damsels' eyes,
For to give a little light,
    When the moon didn't rise.

So, Adam was the first man,
    Eve she was the other.
And Cain walked on the treadmill,
    Because he killed his brother.
Mother Eve couldn't sleep
    Without a downy pillow,
And the greatest man that ever lived
    Was Jack the Giant-killer.

And then they made the sea,
    And in it put a whale,
And then they made a raccoon,
    With rings around his tail.
All the other animals
    Was finished one by one,
And stuck against the fence to dry,
    As fas as they were done.

Oh, lightning is a flashy gal,
   She lives up in the clouds,
And thunder he's a powerful man,
   For he can holler loud.
When he kisses lightning,
   She dodges off in wonder,
Then he jumps and tears his pants,
   And that's what makes the thunder.

Oh, the wind begin to blow,
   And the rain begin to fall,
And the water came so high,
   That it drowned the sinners all.
And it rained forty days and nights,
   Exactly by the counting,
And landed Noah's ark
   'Pon the Alleghany mountains.

Chorus
Then walk in, then walk in, I say,
   Then walk in and hear the banjo play.
Then walk into the parlor,
   And hear the banjo ring,
And watch ol' Cesar's fingers
   While he plays upon the strings.

THE LITTLE OLD LOG CABIN IN THE LANE

I'm getting old and feeble now,

   I cannot work no more.

I've laid de rusty-bladed hoe to rest,

   Ol' Massa and Missis am dead.

Dey're sleepin' side by side,

   Deir spirits now are roamin' wid de blest.

De scene am changed about de place,

   De darkies am all gone,

I nebber hear dem singin' in de cane.

   An' I'se de only one dat's left,

Wid dis ol' dog ob mine,

   In de little ol' log cabin in de lane.

Chorus

De chimney's fallin' down an' de roof is cavin' in,

   I ain't got long around here to remain.

But de angels watches over me when I lays down to sleep,

   In de little ol' log cabin in de lane.

CLIMBING UP THE GOLDEN STAIRS

(Fiddle tune on page 38)

Come, all you little niggers,

Now watch your cues and figures,

Climbing up the golden stairs.

If they think you are a dude,

They will treat you rather rude,

Climbing up the golden stairs!

Old Peter looked so wicked,

When I asked him for a ticket,

Climbing up the golden stairs!

At the sight of half a dollar,

He will grab you by the collar,

And fire you up the golden stairs!

283

Old Satan's not a dandy,
  To feed you sugar candy,
Climbing up the golden stairs.
  But he'll give you brimstone hot,
And he'll choke you on the spot,
  Climbing up the golden stairs!

They'll lock you in the stable,
  Make you fight for Cain and Abel,
Climbing up the golden stairs!
  Old man Adam and his wife,
Will be there with drum and fife,
  To march you up the golden stairs!

Go tell——
  The sights would knock — silly,
Climbing up the golden stairs!
  And tell——
He must be a better man,
  If he'd climb the golden stairs!

—— 's respected,
  But he's bound to be rejected,
Climbing up the golden stairs!
  Oh, you bet he'll kick and yell!
When they fire him into — well,
  Climbing up the golden stairs.

Chorus

Then hear them bells a-ringing,
  'Tis sweet, I do declare.
Oh, hear them darkies singing,
  Climbing up the golden stairs!

284

LUCKY JIM

Jim and I as boys grew up together,
   All the days kind fortune smiled on him.
Brightly through life's dark and stormy weather,
   The folks, they used to call him Lucky Jim.

As chums we shared our fortunes with each other,
   By chance we found we loved the same sweet maid.
They were married, I could find no other,
   Jim was happy, I a bachelor stayed.

Years rolled on, poor Jim passed on to heaven,
   With grief and sorrow in his grave was laid.
When time drug by I married his dear widow,
   Jim was lucky, I unlucky stayed.

Chorus

Ah, lucky Jim, how I envied him,
Ah, lucky Jim, how I envied him!

JENNIE JOHNSON

Went down South to see my gal.

    Hi, Jennie, Ho, Jennie,

    Hey, Jennie Johnson.

She's as fat as old aunt Sal.

    Hi, Jennie, Ho, Jennie,

    Hey, Jennie Johnson.

'Possum souse and mustard greens.

    Hi, Jennie, Ho, Jennie,

    Hey, Jennie Johnson.

Old corn-dodger, pork and beans.

    Hi, Jennie, Ho, Jennie,

    Hey, Jennie Johnson.

Went to the hay-loft to find some eggs.

    Hi, Jennie, Ho, Jennie,

    Hey, Jennie Johnson.

Got a big blacksnake 'round my legs.

    Hi, Jennie, Ho, Jennie,

    Hey, Jennie Johnson.

Jug in the manger, under the hay.
  Hi, Jennie, Ho, Jennie,
  Hey, Jennie Johnson.
The mules got drunk and ran away.
  Hi, Jennie, Ho, Jennie,
  Hey, Jennie Johnson.

Ridin' to Alabam' to make a call.
  Hi, Jennie, Ho, Jennie,
  Hey, Jennie Johnson.
Won't get back till 'way next fall.
  Hi, Jennie, Ho, Jennie,
  Hey, Jennie Johnson.

Chorus

J-e-n-n-i-e J-o-h-n-s-o-n,
  Hi, Jennie, Ho, Jennie,
  Hey, Jennie Johnson.
J-e-n-n-i-e J-o-h-n-s-o-n,
  Hi, Jennie, Ho, Jennie,
  Hey, Jennie Johnson.

MY NELLIE'S BLUE EYES
(Waltz Song)

My dear Nellie's eyes are blue, hair of bright and golden hue,

    Like her heart, her eyes are true, my Nellie, my own.

Never lived a queen so fair, with my Nellie life I'd share,

    By her side I know no care, my Nellie, my own.

Ne'er was culled from nature's bow'r half so rare or sweet a flower,

    Tho' we've culled them hour by hour, my Nellie, my own.

When I first saw Nellie's home, where the moonbeams softly shone,

From my heart a lover's moan, my Nellie, my own.

Fairer seem'd this world to me, whilst the wind blew o'er the lea,

Words and kisses sweet for me, my Nellie, my own.

Like a rose refreshed with dew, my sad heart when won by you,

Angel words said: "Thou art true!" my Nellie, my own.

Chorus

My Nellie's blue eyes, my Nellie's blue eyes,

Brighter than stars shine at night, my Nellie's blue eyes.

DANCING IN THE BARN
(See also "Dancin' on de Green" on page 398)

Oh, we'll meet at de ball in de evenin',
 'Kase I love to pass de time away,
With Clementina Consitina,
 And my Angemima Mina May.
Den we'll balance all to one another,
 Like de ship dat's goin' round de Horn,
Dar we'll meet you, yes, we'll greet you,
 While dancin' in de barn.

Den we's off to work in de mornin',
 Singin' as we go out to de field,
Pickin' cotton, all else forgotten,
 Except to see how much de ground do yield.
De black folks are happy while together,
 It's funny for to hear dem tell a yarn,
About a lover, with kisses smother,
 While dancin' in de barn.

Chorus

As we move so gracefully, we're happy as can be.
 Den swing your partners all together,
'Kase now's de time for you to learn.
 Banjo's ringin', darkies singin' and dancin' in de barn.

DADDY

Take my head on your shoulder, Daddy,
  Turn your face to the West.
It is just the hour when the sky turns gold,
  The hour that Mother loves best.
The day has been long without you, Daddy,
  You've been such a while away,
And you're as tired of your work, Daddy,
  As I am tired of my play.

But I've got you and you've got me,
  So everything seems right.
I wonder if Mother is thinking of us,
  Because it's my birthday night.

Why do your big tears fall, Daddy?
  Mother's not far away,
I often seem to hear her voice,
  Falling across my play.

And it sometimes makes me cry, Daddy,
  To think it's none of it true.
Till I fall asleep to dream, Daddy,
  Of home and Mother and you.
For I've got you and you've got me,
  So everything may go.
We're all the world to each other, Daddy
  For Mother, dear Mother, once told me so.

GOOD BYE, LIZA JANE

The time has come an' I must go,

I must play on the old banjo.

Walk, Dad Lew! Oh, Mister Lew!

Ehe! ehe! he! Hear me now.

The time has come, I do declare,

I want a lock of my girl's hair.

Walk, Dad Lew! Oh, Mister Lew!

Ehe! ehe! he! Hear me now.

Behind the hen-house, on my knees,
　Thought I heard a chicken sneeze.
Walk, Dad Lew! Oh, Mister Lew!
　Ehe! ehe! he! Hear me now.
'Twas nothin' but a rooster sayin' his prayers,
　And givin' out a hymn: "Such a gettin' upstairs."
Walk, Dad Lew! Oh, Mister Lew!
　Ehe! ehe! he! Hear me now.

Chickens and hens have gone to roost,
　Hawk flew down and bit a goose.
Walk, Dad Lew! Oh, Mister Lew!
　Ehe! ehe! he! Hear me now.
He bit a duck in the middle of the back,
　Made the old drake go quack, quack, quack.
Walk, Dad Lew! Oh, Mister Lew!
　Ehe! ehe! he! Hear me now.

Chorus

I'm goin' away to leave you,
　So, good-bye, good-bye.
I'm goin' away to leave you,
　So, good-bye, Liza Jane!
I'm goin' away to leave you,
　I'm goin' to Lynchburg town,
If you get there before I do,
　It's good-bye, Liza Jane!

WHOA, MULE, WHOA!

(See also another version of "Whoa! Mule, Whoa!" on page 440)

I went up on the mountain,
    To give my horn a blow.
I looked down on the other side,
    And there I saw my beau.

I went up to see Miss Liza
    She was standing in the door.
Shoes and stockins' in her hand,
    And feet all over the floor.

I asked Miss Liza for a kiss.
    Now, reckon what she did?
She picked up a chunk of stovewood,
    And hit me on the head.

I carried Miss Liza to the parson's.
    Miss Liza, you keep cool.
I shore would like to kiss you,
    But I'm busy with this mule.

Whoa, mule, whoa!

Whoa, mule, I say!

Just hop right in, Miss Liza,

And hold on to the sleigh.

I WISH I WUZ A LITTLE ROCK

I wish't I wuz a little rock,

A-sittin' on a hill,

An' doin' nothin' all day long

But jus' a-sittin' still.

I wouldn't eat, I wouldn't sleep,

I wouldn't even wash!

But jus' set still a million years,

An' res' myself, by gosh!

THE PARLOR
(See also "Father's Whiskers" on page 434)

The light is in the parlor,
    The fire is in the grate,
The clock upon the mantel,
    Ticks out it's getting late.
The curtains at the windows,
    Are made of snowy white,
The parlor is a pleasant place,
    To sit in Sunday night.

There's books upon the table,
    There's pictures on the wall,
And there's a pretty sofa,
    But the sofa isn't all.
If I am not mistaken,
    I'm sure that I am right,
I see somebody sitting there,
    This pleasant Sunday night.

There's someone on the sofa,
    At first I cannot see,
How many's on the sofa,
    But I don't think there are three.
The clock upon the mantel,
    Ticks out with all its might,
The parlor is a pleasant place,
    To sit in Sunday night.

The light is burning dimly,
The fire is getting low,
When somebody says to somebody else,
"It's time for me to go."
And then I hear a whisper,
So gentle and so light;
"Oh, don't forget to come again,
Another Sunday night!"

GUM TREE CANOE

On Tombigbee river so bright I was born,
 In a hut made of husks of the tall yellow corn.
And there I first met with my Julia so true,
 And I rowed her about in my gum tree canoe.

All day in the field the soft cotton I hoe,
 I think of my Julia and sing as I go.
Oh, I'll catch her a bird with a wing of true blue,
 And at night sail her round in my gum tree canoe.

With my hands on the banjo and toe on the oar,
 I'll sing to the sound of the river's soft roar.
While the stars they look down on my Julia so true,
 And dance in her eyes in my gum tree canoe.

One night the stream bore us so far away,
 That we couldn't come back, so we thought we'd just
  stay.
Oh, we spied a tall ship with a flag of true blue,
 And it took us in tow with my gum tree canoe.

Chorus

Singing, row away, row, o'er the waters so blue,
Like a feather we'll float, in my gum tree canoe.

PREACHER AND THE BEAR

Chorus

1st Chorus   *2nd Chorus*

A colored preacher went out a-hunting.

   It was on a Sunday morn.

Of course, it was against his religion,

   But he took his gun along.

He shot himself some very fine quail,

   A 'possum, a duck and a hare,

And, on the way returning to his home,

   He met a great big grizzly bear.

300

The bear marched out into the middle of the road,

    The better his victim to see,

And the parson got so excited

    That he climbed a persimmon tree.

That bear reared up and he shook that tree,

    But the parson held on with vim,

And he rolled his eyes toward the Ruler of the skies,

    And these words prayed to Him:

Chorus

"Oh, Lawd, you deliv'ed li'l' Dan'el frum de lion's den.

Li'l' Jonah frum de belly ob de whale, an' den,

De Hebrew chillun frum de fi'y fu'nace,

De good book do decleah.

Now, Lawd, ef'n you kain' he'p me,

Fo' goodness sake doan he'p dat beah!"

Spoken

PREACHER. "Now, Mist' Beah, le's you an' me reason dis out, hunh?"

BEAR. "G-r-r-r-r!"

PREACHER. "Nice ol' beah."

BEAR. "G-r-r-r-r-r!"

PREACHER. "Good ol' beah."

BEAR. "G-R-R-R-R-R-R!"

PREACHER. "Ef'n Ah kem down an' let y'all tek jes' one li'l' bite, den would yeh gwan 'way an' leabe me 'lone?"

BEAR. "G-r-r-r-r-e-e-ah!"

PREACHER. "Oh, yeh would, hey? H-e-e-e-ha! Well, Ah's gwine teh stay right up heah whah Ah is."

The preacher sat up there thinking:

"What will ma congagation say,
Ef'n dey should heah dat wuthy pahson Brown
    Went huntin' on de Sabbef day?"

He climbed higher up into the tree,
    In hopes some help to call,
But the limb broke loose from under his feet
    And the parson began to fall.

The bear looked up and he frothed at the mouth,
    As the parson came tumbling down,
But the parson got out his razor,
    Before he hit the ground.

The bear began to growl and the parson to shout,
    Till they made an awful din,
And he cast his eyes toward the Ruler of the skies,
    And once more prayed to Him:

Chorus

"Oh, Lawd, you deliv'ed li'l' Dan'el frum de lion's den.
Li'l' Jonah frum de belly ob de whale, an' den,
De Hebrew chillun frum de fi'y fu'nace,
De scripters do recite.
Now, Lawd, ef'n you doan he'p dat beah
You's gwine teh see a pow'ful fight!"

KISS ME QUICK AND GO

The other night while I was sparking,

    Sweet Tarlina Spray,

The more we whispered our love talking,

    The more we had to say.

The old folks and the little folks,

    We thought were fast in bed.

We heard a footstep on the stairs,

    And what do you think she said?

Soon after that I gave my love

    A moonlight promenade.

At last we fetched up to our door,

    Just where the old folks stayed.

The clock struck twelve, my heart struck too,

    And peeping overhead,

We saw a nightcap raise the blind,

    And what do you think she said?

Chorus

Oh, kiss me quick and go!

My honey, kiss me quick and go!

To cheat surprise and prying eyes,

Why, kiss me quick and go!

GOOD-BYE, MY LOVER, GOOD-BYE

(Parody, "Bought a Rooster" on page 442)

The ship goes sailing down the bay,

Good-bye, my lover, good-bye!

We may not meet for many a day,

Good-bye, my lover, good-bye!

My heart will evermore be true,
    Though now we sadly say adieu.
Oh, kisses sweet I leave with you,
    Good-bye, my lover, good-bye!

I'll miss you on the stormy deep,
    Good-bye, my lover, good-bye!
What can I do but ever weep?
    Good-bye, my lover, good-bye!
My heart is broken with regret,
    But never dream that I'll forget.
I loved you once, I love you yet,
    Good-bye, my lover, good-bye!

Chorus

The ship goes sailing down the bay,
    Good-bye, my lover, good-bye!
'Tis sad to tear my heart away.
    Good-bye, my lover, good-bye!

THE FORTY ACRE FARM

I'm thinking wife, of neighbor Jones, that man with stalwart arm.
  He lives in peace and plenty on a forty acre farm.
When men are all around us with hearts and hands a-sore,
  Who own two hundred acres and still are wanting more.

No weeds are in the cornfield, no thistles in the oats,
  The horses show good keeping by their fine and glossy coats.
The cows within the meadow beneath the beachen shade,
  Learn all their gentle manners from a gentle milking maid.

Within the field on Saturday he leaves no cradled grain,
  To be gathered on the morrow for fear of coming rain.
He keeps the Sabbath holy, his children learn his ways;
  He fills his barns with plenty at the close of harvest days.

May we not learn a lesson, wife, from prudent neighbor Jones
  And not for what we haven't got give vent to sighs and groans?
The rich ain't always happy nor free from life's alarms,
  But blest be those who live content though small may be their
    farms.

SWEET MEMORIES OF THEE

When soft stars are peeping thro' the pure azure sky
   And southern gales sweeping their warm breathings by,
Like sweet music praling far o'er the blue sea,
   Then came o'er me stealing, sweet mem'ries of thee.

The bright rose, when faded, flings forth o'er the tomb
   Its velvet leaves laded with silent perfume.
Then round me will hover in grief or in glee,
   Till life's dream be over, sweet mem'ries of thee.

As a sweet lute lingers in silence alone,
   Unswept by light fingers scarce murmers a tone,
My young heart resembles that lute light and free,
   Till o'er its chords tremble those mem'ries of thee.

KITTY CLOVER

Sweet Kitty Clover she bother'd me so, oh! oh! oh! oh!
  Sweet Kitty Clover she bother'd me so, oh! oh! oh! oh!
Her face is round and red and fat,
  Like a pulpit cushion or redder than that, Oh!

Sweet Kitty in person is rather low, oh! oh! oh! oh!
  Oh sweet Kitty Clover you bother me so, oh! oh! oh! oh!
She's three feet tall and that I prize,
  As just a fit wife for a man of my size, Oh!

Where Kitty resides I'm sure to go, oh! oh! oh! oh!
  Oh sweet Kitty Clover you bother me so, oh! oh! oh! oh!
One moonlight night, ah, me what bliss.
  Through a hole in a window I gave her a kiss, Oh!

If Kitty to Kirk with me would go, oh! oh! oh! oh!
  Then Kitty would ne'er again bother me so, oh! oh! oh! oh!
I think I should never be wretched again
  If after the parson she'd say amen.

YOU NEVER MISS THE WATER TILL THE WELL
RUNS DRY

(Waste not, want not)

When a child I lived at Lincoln with my parents on the farm.

The lessons that my mother taught to me were quite a charm.

She would often take me on her knee when tired of childish play,

And as she pressed me to her breast I've heard my mother say:

As years rolled on I grew to be a mischief-making boy.

Destruction seemed my only sport, it was my only joy.

And well do I remember when — ofttimes well chastised,

How father sat beside me then and thus has me advised:

When I arrived at manhood I embarked in public life,

And found it was a rugged road, bestrewn with care and strife.

I speculated foolishly, my losses were severe,

But still a tiny little voice kept whispering in my ear:

Then I studied strict economy and found to my surprise,
  My funds instead of sinking very quickly then did rise.
I grasped each chance and always struck the iron while it was hot;
  I seized my opportunities and never once forgot:

I'm married now and happy; I've a careful little wife.
  We live in peace and harmony, devoid of care and strife.
Fortune smiles upon us, we have little children three.
  The lessons that I teach them as they prattle round my knee:

Chorus

Waste not, want not, is a maxim I would teach.
  Let your watchword be dispatch, and practise what you preach.
Do not let your chances, like sunbeams, pass you by,
  For you never miss the water till the well runs dry.

ROBINSON CRUSOE
(Fiddle tune, "Poor Old Robinson Crusoe" on page 79)

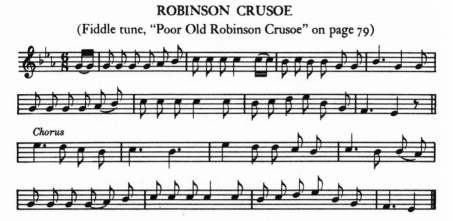

When I was a lad I had cause to be sad,
    A very good friend I did lose, oh!
I warrant you, Dan, you have heard of this man,
    His name it was Robinson Crusoe.

Chorus

Oh, Robinson Crusoe! Oh, poor Robinson Crusoe!
He went off to sea and, between you and me,
Old Neptune wrecked Robinson Crusoe.

But he saved from a-board an old gun and a sword
    And another old matter or two, so
By dint of his thrift he just managed to shift
    And keep alive Robinson Crusoe.

Chorus

Oh, Robinson Crusoe! Oh, poor Robinson Crusoe!
Whether tempest or Turk, or wild man or work,
No matter to Robinson Crusoe.

The cannibals came to his island one day
   To feast, for all cannibals do so,
But Friday, their man, jumped out of the pan,
   And ran off to Robinson Crusoe.

Chorus

Oh, Robinson Crusoe! Oh, poor Robinson Crusoe!
He fired off his gun, and then there was fun
For lonely old Robinson Crusoe.

But he never lost hope, and he never would mope,
   And he always had faith, as should you, so
That come as it might, it always was right
   With honest old Robinson Crusoe.

Chorus

Oh, Robinson Crusoe! Oh, poor Robinson Crusoe!
Where can school-boy be found, to stop at a round?
"Hurrah for old Robinson Crusoe!"

WHERE WAS MOSES WHEN THE LIGHT WENT OUT?

When a child I used to go to bed at eight each night.

The nurse girl used to frighten me when she put out the light.

She'd talk of ghosts and goblins in a very awful way,

She'd then put out the candle and to me she used to say:

Now Moses being my Christian name, I used to feel afraid,

And dreading something awful, I for hours have laid.

Sometimes I'd cry myself to sleep, but horrid things I dreamed,

For naughty ghosts at my bedside glared at me while they
screamed:

Upon the nurse I spit, and she was kindly asked to leave,

But Moses Muggins married her, for which we did not grieve.

I met her in the street when she had just two days been wed,

And didn't she warm my jacket, when I innocently said:

Some twenty years passed by before I heard the phrase again:
  Alone with a young lady, I was riding in a train.
We rushed into a tunnel, and when all was pitchy dark
  My lovely little lady friend gave vent to this remark:

Now when once more the light of day we saw, to her I said,
  "As you've wakened up old memories, you're the girl I'd like to
      wed."
We're married now, and six fine boys amuse us every night,
  And sing this jolly chorus, when their Pa puts out the light:

Chorus
"Where was Moses when the light went out?
  Where was Moses? What was he about?
Now my little man, tell me if you can,
  Where was Moses when the light went out?"

THE CAMPBELLS ARE COMING
(Fiddle tune, "The Campbells are Coming," on page 110)

The Campbells are comin', O ho, O ho,
 The Campbells are comin', O ho, O ho!
The Campbells are comin' to bonnie Lochleven,
 The Campbells are comin', O ho, O ho!

Upon the Lomonds I lay, I lay,
 Upon the Lomonds I lay, I lay,
I looked down to bonnie Lochleven
 And heard three bonnie pipers play.

The great Argyle, he goes before,
 He makes his cannon loudly roar;
Wi' sound of trumpet, pipe and drum,
 The Campbells are comin', O ho, O ho!

The Campbells they are a' in arms,
 Their loyal faith and truth to show;
Wi' banners rattlin' in the wind,
 The Campbells are comin', O ho, O ho!

315

GRANDMA'S ADVICE

My Grandma lives on yonder little green,
   Fine old lady as ever was seen.
She often cautioned me with care,
   Of all false young men to beware.
Tim-e-i tim-e-um tum tim-e-um pa ta,
   Of all false young men to beware.

These false young men they flatter and deceive,
   So, my love, you must not believe.
They'll flatter, they'll coax, till you are in their snare,
   And away goes poor old grandma's care.
Tim-e-i tim-e-um tum tim-e-um pa ta,
   And away goes poor old grandma's care.

The first came a courting was little Johny Green,
    Fine young man as ever was seen;
But the words of my Grandma ran in my head,
    And I could not hear one word he said.
Tim-e-i tim-e-um tum tim-e-um pà ta,
    And I could not hear one word he said.

The next came a courting was young Ellis Grove,
    'Twas then we met with a joyous love;
With a joyous love I couldn't be afraid,
    You'd better get married than die an old maid.
Tim-e-i tim-e-um tum tim-e-um pa ta,
    You'd better get married than die an old maid.

Thinks I to myself, there's some mistake:
    What a fuss these old folks make!
If the boys and the girls had all been so afraid,
    Then grandma herself would have died an old maid.
Tim-e-i tim-e-um tum tim-e-um pa ta,
    Then grandma herself would have died an old maid.

TWENTY YEARS AGO

I've wandered to the village, Tom, I've sat beneath the tree,
  Upon the schoolhouse playing ground which sheltered you and
    me.
But none were there to greet me, Tom, and few were left to know,
  That played with us upon the green some twenty years ago.

The grass is just as green, dear Tom, barefooted boys at play
  Were sporting just as we did then with spirits just as gay;
But the Master sleeps upon the hill which, coated o'er with snow,
  Afforded us a sliding place just twenty years ago.

The old school-house is altered some, the benches are replaced
  By new ones very like the ones our penknives had defaced;
But the same old logs are in the walls, the bell swings to and fro,
  The music just the same, dear Tom, 'twas twenty years ago.

The boys are playing some old game, beneath the same old tree;
  I do forget the name just now — you've played it there with me,
On that same spot, 'twas played with knives, by throwing so and so—
  The losers had a task to do then, twenty years ago.

The river's running just as still, the willows on its side
  Are larger than they were, dear Tom, the stream appears less
    wide.
The grape-vine swing is ruined, now, where once we played the
    beau,
  And swung our sweethearts, "pretty girls," just twenty years ago.

The spring that bubbled 'neath the hill close by the spreading
    beech,
  Is very low, 'twas once so high that we could almost reach;
And kneeling down to get a drink, dear Tom, I started so
  To see how much that I had changed since twenty years ago.

Near by the spring, upon an elm, you know I cut your name,
  Your sweetheart's just beneath it, Tom, and you did mine the
    same;
Some heartless wretch had peeled the bark, 'twas dying sure but
    slow,
  Just as that one, whose name was cut, died twenty years ago.

My lids have long been dry, dear Tom, but tears came in my eyes;
  I thought of her I loved so well, those early broken ties.
I visited the old church-yard, and took some flowers to strew
  Upon the graves of those we loved some twenty years ago.

Some now are in the church-yard laid, some sleep beneath the sea,
  But few are left of our old class excepting you and me;
And when our time shall come, dear Tom, and we are called to go,
  I hope they'll lay us where we played just twenty years ago.

THE BULL-DOG ON THE BANK

Oh! the bull-dog on the bank
   And the bull-frog in the pool;
Oh! the bull-dog on the bank
   And the bull-frog in the pool;
Oh! the bull-dog on the bank
   And the bull-frog in the pool;
The bull-dog called the bull-frog
   A green old water fool.

Oh! the bull-dog stooped to catch him
   And the snapper caught his paw;
Oh! the bull-dog stooped to catch him
   And the snapper caught his paw;
Oh! the bull-dog stooped to catch him
   And the snapper caught his paw;
The polly-wog died a-laughing
   To see him wag his jaw.

Says the monkey to the owl,
  "O what'll you have to drink?"
Says the monkey to the owl,
  "O what'll you have to drink?"
Says the monkey to the owl,
  "O what'll you have to drink?"
"Since you're so very kind, sir,
  I'll take a bottle of ink."

Pharaoh's daughter on the bank,
  Little Moses in the pool;
Pharaoh's daughter on the bank,
  Little Moses in the pool;
Pharaoh's daughter on the bank,
  Little Moses in the pool;
She fished him out with a ten-foot pole
  And sent him off to school.

WHEN JOHNNY COMES MARCHING HOME

When Johnny comes marching home again,
 Hurrah, hurrah!
We'll give him a hearty welcome then,
 Hurrah, hurrah!
The men will cheer, the boys will shout,
 The ladies, they will all turn out,
And we'll all feel gay
 When Johnny comes marching home.

The old church bell will peal with joy,
    Hurrah, hurrah!
To welcome our darling boy,
    Hurrah, hurrah!
The village lads and lassies say,
    With roses they will strew the way,
And we'll all feel gay
    When Johnny comes marching home.

Get ready for the jubilee,
    Hurrah, hurrah!
We'll give the hero three times three,
    Hurrah, hurrah!
The laurel wreath is ready now
    To place upon his loyal brow;
And we'll all feel gay
    When Johnny comes marching home.

(See also parody, "Three Crows," on page 449)

THE LITTLE MAID MILKING HER COW

Barney, I havn't a moment,
　　So don't you hinder me now
For I'm in haste to the meadow;
　　I'm going to milk the cow.

Why are you wandering here, sir,
　　And just at the break of day?
You knew I was coming a milking,
　　Now I bid you keep out of the way.

It's just your bold way of actin';
　　See how you follow me now;
Coming here and distractin';
　　A little maid milking her cow.

How can I milk when you're near me
  If you bewilder me so,
Discoursin' nonsense and blarney,
  And stay when I bid you to go?

And see, now, you're standing beside me;
  Be careful, I beg and pray;
The cow, sure, is close to you, listening,
  And minds every word that you say.

And 'tis herself is remarkin'
  The way you're going on now;
She wonders you'll keep on distractin'
  A little maid milking her cow.

You sigh it's darkness about ye,
  That I'm the light of your day;
You vow you can't live without me;
  Sure, that's what the other boys say.

Well, take up the pail, and we'll go now
  And homeward we'll wend our way.
Who knows, if you're not too consaited,
  The mother may hear you today?

And may be I'll whisper you've told me,
  With solemn promise and vow,
That you'll be kind to her Colleen,
  The little maid milking her cow.

McSORLEY'S TWINS

Arrah! Mrs. McSorley had fine purty twins,

Two fat little divels they were.

Wid shquallin' and bawlin' from mornin' till night,

It would deafen you, I do declare.

Be me soul 'twas a caution the way they would schream.

Like the blast of a fireman's horn.

Says McSorley: "Not wan blissid hour have I shlept,

Since them two little divils was born."

Says Mrs. McSorley: "A christenin' we'll have,

Just to give me two darlins' a name."

"Faith, we will," says McSorley, "sure one they must get,

Somethin' grand too, becourse for that same."

Thin for godmothers Kate and Mag Murphy stood up,
  And for godfathers came the two Flynns.
Johanna Maria and Diagnacious O'Mara,
  Were the names they christened the twins.

Chorus

Wid the beer and the whiskey the whole blessed night,
  Faith they couldn't sthand up on their pins.
Such an illigant time at the christenin' we had,
  Of McSorley's most beautiful twins.

I WISH I WAS SINGLE AGAIN

Oh, when I was single, oh then, oh then,
  Oh, when I was single, oh then.
Oh, when I was single my pockets would jingle
  And I wish I was single again.

I took me a wife, oh then, oh then,
  I took me a wife, oh then.
I took me a wife, she was the joy of my life,
  But now I am single again.

My wife she died, oh then, oh then,
  My wife she died, oh then.
My wife she died, and oh, how I cried,
  And then I was single again.

I married another, oh then, oh then,
  I married another, oh then.
I married another, she's the Divil's grandmother,
  And I wish I was single again.

BLOW, BOY, BLOW

Blow, my bullies, I long to hear you,
  Blow, boys, blow!
Blow, my bullies, I come to cheer you,
  Blow, my bully boys, blow!

A Yankee ship's gone down the river,
  Blow, boys, blow!
And what do you think they got for supper?
  Old sow-bosom and beans!

BLOW THE MAN DOWN

As I was walking down Paradise Street,
  Way! Hey! Blow the man down!
A pretty young damsel I chanced to meet,
  Give me some time to blow the man down.

Says she to me: "Will you stand treat?"
  Way! Hey! Blow the man down!
"Delighted," says I, "for a charmer so sweet."
  Give me some time to blow the man down.

KEEP THAT 'POSSUM WARM

Peter, you come in to dinner.
  Can't you wait till I hoe this row?
Come along here, you wicked sinner,
  Can't you wait till I hoe this row?

329

Keep that 'possum warm,

Keep that 'possum warm,

Keep that 'possum warm,

And wait till I hoe this row.

(See above verses in Negro dialect on page 18)

PUT ME IN MY LITTLE BED

Chorus

Oh, birdie, I am tired now,

 I do not care to hear you sing.

You've sung your happy songs all day,

 Now put your head beneath your wing.

I'm sleepy, too, as I can be,

 And, sister, when my prayer is said,

I want to lay me down and rest,

 So put me in my little bed.

Oh, sister, what did mother say,
  When she was called to heaven away?
She told me always to be good,
  And never, never go astray.
I can't forget the day she died,
  She placed her hand upon my head,
And whispered softly: "Keep my child."
  And then they told me she was dead.

Dear sister, come and hear my prayer,
  Now, ere I lay me down to sleep,
Within my. heavenly Father's care,
  While angels bright their vigils keep.
And let me ask of Him above,
  To keep my soul in paths of right.
Oh, let me thank Him for His love,
  Ere I shall say my last good-night.

Chorus

Come, sister, come kiss me good-night,
  For I my evening prayer have said.
I'm tired now, and sleepy too,
  Come, put me in my little bed.

A LITTLE MORE CIDER TOO

I love the white girl and the black,
And I love all the rest.
I love the girls for loving me,
But I love myself the best.
Oh dear, I am so thirsty,
I've just been down to supper,
I drunk three pails of apple-jack,
And a tub of apple butter.

When I first saw Miss Snowflake,
'Twas on Broadway I spied her,
I'd give my hat and boots, I would,
If I could be beside her.
She looked at me, I looked at her,
And then I crossed the street,
And then she smiled and said to me:
"A little more cider, sweet."

Oh! I wish I was an apple
   And Snowflake was another.
Oh! what a pretty pair we'd make
   Upon a tree together.
How bad the darkies all would feel
   When on the tree they spied her,
To think how luscious we would be
   When we're made into cider.

But now old age comes creeping,
   We grow down and don't get bigger,
And cider sweet, am sour then,
   And I am just de nigger.
But let the cause be what it will,
   Short, small, or wider,
She am the apple of my eye
   And I'm bound to be beside 'er.

Oh, a little more cider too,
   Oh, a little more cider too,
Oh a little more cider for Miss Dinah,
   A little more cider too.

THE WIDOW IN THE COTTAGE BY THE SEA

Just one year ago today, love,
  I became your happy bride.
Changed a mansion for a cottage,
  To dwell by the riverside.
You told me I'd be happy,
  But no happiness I see,
For tonight I am a widow,
  In a cottage by the sea.

From my cottage by the seaside,
  I can see my mansion home,
I can see those hills and valleys,
  Where with pleasure I have roamed.
The last time that I met him,
  Oh, how happy then were we!
But tonight I am a widow,
  In the cottage by the sea.

Oh, my poor aged father,
  How in sorrow he would wail,
And my poor and aged mother,
  How in tears her eyes would swell!
And my poor and only brother,
  Oh, how he would weep for me,
If he only knew his sister,
  Was a widow by the sea.

Chorus

Alone, all alone by the seaside he left me,
  And no other's bride I'll be.
For in bridal flowers he decked me,
  In the cottage by the sea.

MAIDEN'S ROMANCE

For a long time to come, I'll remember quite well,
  Alone in a poorhouse a maiden did dwell.
She dwelt with her mother and father serene,
  Her age it was red and her hair was sixteen.

Not far from this maiden her lover did dwell,
  He was knock-kneed in both legs, and hump-backed as well.
He said: "Let us fly by the light of your hair,
  For you are the eye of my apple, so fair."

Said she to this young man: "Now, you just get wise,
  Or the old man will scratch out your nails with his eyes.
If you love me don't leave me, it will be a disgrace!"
  Cried the maid as she buried both mitts in her face.

But when she refused him he rushed at this maid,
  And swiftly he opened the knife of his blade.
And he cut the sweet throat of his maiden so fair,
  And he drug her around by the head of her hair.

And just at this moment the old man arrives,
  And he gazed at his trouble with tears full of eyes.
He knelt by the side of his daughter and kiss't,
  Then he rushed at the youth with both arms full of fist.

Said he to the young man: "Now, you'd better bolt,"

And he drew a horse pistol he'd raised from a colt.

The young man took flight up the chimney 'tis true.

Said he: "I must fly," so he flew up the flue.

BARNEY McCOY

We'll bid all our dear friends good-bye,

We're leaving old Ireland today,

But long for our sweet home we'll sigh,

And weep in the land far away.

The sod of my birth still I love,
   Its mem'ry no pain can destroy,
And true as the stars up above,
   Will be, dear, your Barney McCoy.

The big ship is waiting below,
   And grief fills my soul to depart,
But there we'll meet fortune I know,
   So Nora, my darling, take heart.

'Tis sad to leave mother and home,
   But you are my comfort and joy,
Then say o'er the ocean you'll roam,
   Nor part with your Barney McCoy.

Chorus

Then, dry all your tears, Nora dear!
   Oh, come with your own darling boy!
There's nothing but misery here,
   You'll be happy with Barney McCoy.

THE YEAR OF JUBILO

Chorus

Say, darkies have you seen the massa,
  With the mustache on his face,
Go long the road some time this mornin',
  Like he goin' to leave the place?
He seen the smoke 'way up the river,
  Where the Lincoln gunboats lay,
He took his hat and left very sudden,
  And I 'spect he's run away.

He's six foot one way, two foot t'other,
  And he weighs three hundred pound,
His coat so big he couldn't pay the tailor,
  And it won't go half way round.
He's drilled so much they call him Captain,
  And he got so dreadful tanned,

I 'spect he'll try and fool them Yankees,
   For to think he's contraband.

The darkies feel so lonesome living
   In the log house on the lawn,
They move their things to massa's parlor,
   For to keep it while he's gone.
There's wine and cider in the cellar,
   And the darkies they'll have some,
I s'pose they'll all be confiscated,
   When the Lincoln soldiers come.

Chorus

The massa run? Ha! Ha!
   The darkies stay? Ho! Ho!
It must be now the kingdom comin'
   And the year of Jubilo!

PEEK-A-BOO!

Oh, you ras - cal. there.

On a cold winter's evening when business is done,

And to your home you retire,

What a pleasure it is to have a bright bouncing boy,

One whom you love to admire.

You hug him and kiss him, you press him to your heart,

What joy to your bosom 'twill bring!

Then you place him on the carpet and you'll hide behind the chair,

And to please him you'll commence to sing.

Oh, my heart's always light when at home with my wife,

There joy and peace ever reign.

With my boy on my knee I'm as happy as can be,

I never knew a care or pain.

He's pretty, he's gentle, he's kind and he's good,

And everything nice him I bring.

341

Oh, if he attempts to cry when I am standing by,
  Just to please him I commence to sing.

When the sunshine of youth fades and age bends us low,
  Joys, like the birds, flown away,
Then the smiles of our children ever brighten the path,
  Leading where loved ones do stray.
The music and laughter we ever love to hear,
  Will beam like a rainbow in spring.
By the fireside at night, with our hearts so free and light,
  We will listen while our children sing.

Chorus

Peek-a-boo! Peek-a-boo! Come from behind the chair!
Peek-a-boo! Peek-a-boo! I see you hiding there!

I'SE GWINE TO WEEP NO MORE

De Good Book tells you not to moan,

I'se gwine to weep no more.

Dug dem taters, shuck dat corn,

I'se gwine to weep no more.

Laid my sins away to keep,

   I'se gwine to weep no more.

Laid dem low so dey could sleep,

   I'se gwine to weep no more.

De Jersey Lily's comin' back,

   I'se gwine to weep no more.

Robe me in a sealskin sacque,

   I'se gwine to weep no more.

Deck my breast wid diamond pin,

   I'se gwine to weep no more,

She can chuck me on de chin,

   I'se gwine to weep no more.

Oh, way up yonder in de sky,

   I'se gwine to weep no more.

A roller rinker I can spy,

   I'se gwine to weep no more.

I'll give my wife a soothing drink,

   I'se gwine to weep no more.

To keep her from de roller rink,

   I'se gwine to weep no more.

I've sung you chillun all enuff,

   I'se gwine to weep no more.

De road to Washington am ruff,

   I'se gwine to weep no more.

De days am gone to steal and rob,

   I'se gwine to weep no more,

And many a sinner's lost his job,

I'se gwine to weep no more.

Refrain

Den fare-you-well, I'se gwine for to join dat golden band,

Good-bye, I'se gwine to walk dat golden floor.

I'll take my banjo wid me and I'll touch dat golden harp,

An' I ain't gwine to weep any more!

Chorus

Fare-ye-well!   Fare-ye-well!   I'se gwine to weep no more.

Fare-ye-well!   Fare-ye-well!   I'se gwine to weep no more.

Good-bye!

DEAR KATIE

I was drunk last night, dear Katie,

I was drunk the night before,

And if I live to get sober,

I'll never get drunk any more.

Oh, boys, if you will heed my story,

Corn whisky and gambling are bad.

When you find a true girl you will marry,

Or like me you'll be lonesome and sad.

Dear Katie was sweet as the roses,

Her smile bright as sunshine to me,

Like a flower neglected she faded,

She sleeps 'neath the old chestnut tree.

CARRY ME BACK TO OLD VIRGINNY

(Fiddle tune on page 107)

On the floating scow of old Virginny,

I worked from day to day,

A-raking amongst the oyster beds,

To me it was but play.

346

But now I'm growing very old,
  I cannot work any more,
So carry me back to old Virginny,
  To old Virginny's shore.

If I was only young again,
  I'd lead a different life,
I'd save my money and buy a farm,
  And take Dinah for my wife.
But now old age it holds me tight,
  My limbs are growing sore,
So take me back to old Virginny,
  To old Virginny's shore.

Chorus

Then carry me back to old Virginny,
  To old Virginny's shore.
Oh, carry me back to old Virginny,
  To old Virginny's shore.

I'SE GOIN' TO SAY GOOD-BYE

They say up in the northland,
  Not so many miles away,
The colored folks are flockin'
  'Cause they're gettin' better pay.
My heart am awful heayy,
  And it almost makes me cry,
For when the sun goes down tonight,
  I'se goin' to say good-by!

But Dinah she don't want to go,
  She says: "We're gettin' old,"
She's 'fraid that she will freeze to death,
  The country am so cold.
The story 'bout the work and pay,
  She don't believe it's true,
She begs me not to do anything,
  That I am bound to do.

But now I've sold the cabin,
   And the little patch of ground,
The good old master willed me,
   When the Yankee troops came 'round.
The boat am on the river,
   That's goin' to take me off,
I'se goin' to join the exodus,
   That's startin' for the North.

Chorus

My heart am awful heavy,
   And the tears am in my eyes.
For when the sun goes down to-night,
   I'se goin' to say good-bye!

SWEETHEARTS AND WIVES

'Mid the smiles of bright-eyed lasses,
  And the sight of dear old friends,
When the merry clink of glasses,
  In some jolly chorus blends.
At the cheerful little party,
  With a kind and genial host,
Oft with voices strong and hearty,
  Have we joined in this old toast.

Standing here I see before me,
  Dear old pals I've known for years.
Tho' you're not all married, surely
  You all love the little dears!
Troubles shared are easier carried,
  Wedded life's the happier lot,
Some who're single wish they'd married,
  Some who've married wish they'd not.

Adam soon came to decide,
  He must his lonely life relieve.
Who can tell where you or I'd be,
  But for his fair sweetheart Eve!
Now it follows, but no laughter
  From this Gospel truth evince,
Man came first and woman after —
  She's been after him ever since!

350

Let cold cynics rail at woman,
  They're but ill-conditioned churls.
Be assured that man is no man,
  Who has never cared for girls.
May we love and oft caress them,
  They're the sweetmeats of our lives,
Then let's toast: "The girls —
  God bless them! — first our sweethearts,
Then our wives."

Chorus

Sweethearts and wives, sweethearts and wives!
  Girls are the joy of all our lives!
When pretty lips kiss, oh my, what bliss!
  Who can resist the darlings?

JOHNNY'S SO LONG AT THE FAIR

Oh dear, what can the matter be?
  Dear, dear, what can the matter be?
Oh dear, what can the matter be?
  Johnny's so long at the fair.
He promised to buy me a trinket to please me,
  And for a smile, oh, he vowed he would tease me.
He promised to bring me a bunch of blue ribbons
  To tie up my bonnie brown hair.

Oh dear, what can the matter be?
  Dear, dear, what can the matter be?
Oh dear, what can the matter be?
  Johnny's so long at the fair.
He promised to buy me a basket of posies,
  A garland of lilies, a gift of red roses,
A little straw hat to set off the blue ribbons
  That tie up my bonnie brown hair.

LEAF BY LEAF THE ROSES FALL

Leaf by leaf the roses fall.
  Drop by drop the springs run dry.
One by one beyond recall,
  Summer beauties fade and die.
But the roses bloom again,
  And the springs will gush a-new,
With the springtime's gentle rain
  And the summer's silvery dew.

So in hours of deepest gloom,
  When the springs of gladness fail,
And the roses in their bloom
  Droop like maidens wan and pale;
We shall find some hope that lies
  Like a silent germ apart,
Hidden far from careless eyes,
  In the garden of the heart.

Some sweet hope to gladness wed,
  That will spring afresh and new
When grief's winter shall have fled,
  Giving place to sun and dew.

Some sweet hope that breathes of spring
Through the weary, weary time,
Budding forth its blossoming
In the spirits' silent clime.

LONG TIME AGO!

Near the lake where drooped the willow, long time ago!
　　Where the rock threw back the billow, whiter than snow!
Dwelt a maid beloved and cherished, by high and low!
　　But with autumn's leaf she perished, long time ago!

Rock and tree and flowing water, long time ago!
　　Bird and bee and blossom taught her, love's spell to know!
While to my fond words she listened, murmuring low!
　　Tenderly her blue eyes glistened, long time ago!

Mingled were our hearts forever, long time ago!
　　Can I now forget her? Never! No, lost one, no!
To her grave these tears were given, ever to flow!
　　She's the star I missed from heaven, long time ago!

'WAY OUT WEST IN KANSAS

'Way out West in Kansas,
'Way out West in Kansas,
Grasshoppers eat the wheat,
And leave nothing but the Cheat,
'Way out West in Kansas.

Potatoes they grow small in Kansas,
Potatoes they grow small in Kansas,
Potatoes they grow small,
And we dig 'em in the fall,
And we eat 'em tops and all in Kansas.

Cows give no milk in Kansas,
Cows give no milk in Kansas,
No matter how they try,
The weather is so dry,
They give nothing but a sigh in Kansas.

Pigs never squeal in Kansas,
Pigs never squeal in Kansas,
Pigs never squeal,
They grow skinny as a rail,
And they never curl a tail in Kansas.

Hens don't set in Kansas.

They stay on the roost in Kansas.

The roosters learn to cackle,

And the hens all crow,

They know it's no use in Kansas.

Farming don't pay in Kansas,

Farming don't pay in Kansas,

The chickens never lay,

And the rabbits eat the hay,

Farming don't pay in Kansas.

I don't want to dwell in Kansas,

I don't want to dwell in Kansas,

I don't want to dwell,

Through the long dry spell,

Where the farmer catches hell in Kansas.

Never take a claim in Kansas,

Never take a claim in Kansas,

Never take a claim,

It will whip you in the main,

If you don't go insane in Kansas.

Those who first took claims in Kansas had many trials and tribulations, according to this song. It might well be entitled "The Homesteader's Lament." However, like all true pioneers, though heartbreaking misfortune was their lot, they made the best of a bad adventure. And, in the parlance of today, they could really "take it." Their hardiness was shown, even in their retreat from the sun-scorched plains of Kansas, by their sense of humor, which was represented by signs printed on their covered-wagons, such as:

Bleeding Kansas, we bid you adieu.

We may emigrate to hell but never back to you.

Another one was:

Of all places in the whole creation,

Kansas is nearest to hell and damnation.

If we manage to find a railroad station,

We're going back East to my wife's relation.

Another one had still worse luck:

I et my boots and the saddle leather.

The old woman's thin and light as a feather.

The young 'uns all sick and so am I.

What we hyer'd about Kansas was all a dam'd lie.

This one had a cow and a mule hitched to his wagon:

One mule's deader 'n a nail, by God.

He died from a belly-full of Kansas sod.

This covered-wagon poetry was originated by the "Injun" traders about a decade before the influx of the homesteaders into Kansas. With ox-teams and covered wagons loaded with "tradin'" goods, these traders treked across the Kansas plains to Colorado and points West. Outgoing wagons were decorated with poetry or slogans, such as: "Pike's Peak or Bust!" Many of the returning wagons bore the legend: "Busted, by God!"

However, in spite of earlier defeats, the indomitable will of the hardy homesteaders prevailed, and Kansas became one of the bright stars in the nation's flag.

OH, I SHOULD LIKE TO MARRY

Gent.   Oh, I should like to marry, if that I could find,
       Any pretty lady suited to my mind.
  Oh, I should like her witty, oh, I should like her good,
    With a little money, oh, yes, indeed I should.

Lady.   Oh, I should like to marry, if that I could find,
       Any handsome fellow suited to my mind.
  Oh, I should like him dashing, oh, I should like him gay,
    The leader of the fashion and dandy of the day.

Gent.   Oh, I should like her hair to cluster like the vine,
    I should like her eyes to look like sparkling wine,
  And let her brows resemble Diana's crescent.
    Let her voice, to me, be always soft and pleasant.

Lady.   Oh, I should like his hair as Truffi's wigs divine,
      The sort of thing each fair would envy, being mine!
  He mustn't be too short, he mustn't be too burly,
    But slim and tall and straight, with moustache and
                             whiskers curly.

Gent.   Oh, let her feet be nearly like to the Chinese,

Who little feet to make, in wooden shoes do squeeze.
Oh, let her form be upright, both elegant and free,
With a gentle temper, oh, then we shall agree.

Lady.   His cab, too, he must drive with a tiny tiger dear,
And a phaeton and a brougham and ten thousand
pounds a year!
He mustn't wish to have all things just his way.
He must mope when I am grave and be gay when I am
gay.

Gent.   Oh, now, my fair young ladies, do not be unkind,
For it would be a favor, such a one to find.
And now I'll bid adieu and bless you all, I say.
And if you don't object, we'll meet another day.

Lady.   I'm sure he'll never grumble, but live a life of ease.
That is, on one condition, I'm to do whate'er I please!
Now isn't this good natured and don't you all agree,
This tiny little privilege is not too much for me.

Come, boys, I have something to tell you,
   Come here, I will whisper it low.
You're thinking of leaving the homestead.
   Don't be in a hurry to go.
The city has many attractions,
   But think of its vices and sins.
When once in the vortex of fashion,
   How soon our destruction begins!

You talk of the mines of Nevada,
   They're wealthy in treasure no doubt.
But, ah, there is gold in the farm, boys,
   If only you'll shovel it out.
The mercantile life is a hazard
   Surrounded by glitter and show,
And wealth is not made in a day, boys,
   Don't be in a hurry to go.

361

The farm is the best and the safest,
   And certainly surest to pay,
You're free as the air of the mountain,
   And monarch of all you survey.
Then stay on the farm a while longer,
   Tho' profits come in rather slow.
Remember you've nothing to risk, boys,
   Don't be in a hurry to go.

Chorus

Stay on the farm, stay on the farm,
   Tho' profits come in rather slow.
Stay on the farm, stay on the farm,
   Don't be in a hurry to go.

HANDSOME HARRY

Handsome Harry, handsome Harry Thomas,
  He was sued, yes, sued for breach of promise.
He took Mary walking thro' the dell
  And Mary promised not to tell.
Mary went right home and told her mother.
  Ma told Pa, and Pa told her brother.
Brother told the preacher, and
  The preacher tolled the wedding bells.

363

Never take a walk with Mary,
   Never take a walk with Sue,
Never take a walk with Maud or Carrie,
   That's the kind of girl you'll have to marry.
When you want to go out walking,
   Strolling thro' the shady dell,
Always take a girl named Daisy,
   'Cause daisies don't tell.

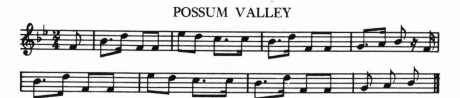

In Possum valley there doth dwell
 A comely lass I know full well.
Her home is in a pleasant dell.
 The sweet one's name is Mollie Ell!

Yet I am sorely grieved to think
 She brought me nigh to ruin's brink.
In telling me my hope is vain,
 That she will never love a swain.

Ah me! Poor me! I am undone,
 She has my heart and I have none.
Now heartless I the world must roam,
 An exile, banished from her home!

But do not think that I will grieve,
 Nor sadly thus my heart deceive,
In thinking I no more can find
 A maiden suited to my mind.

No, rather than be such a fool,
 I'll drown myself in a dry pool.
Or hang myself by the great toes,
 To be a scarecrow for the crows.

And now to you a kind farewell,
   My sweet, my dearest, Mollie Ell,
Hoping that you indeed may find
   A lover suited to your mind.

SANDY SAM AND RUSTY JIGGS

Away up in the Sierry Peaks,
  Where the mountain pines grow tall,
Sandy Sam and Rusty Jiggs
  Had a round-up camp last fall.

They had their ponies and their running irons,
  And maybe a dog or two,
And they 'lowed they'd brand every slick-eared dogie
  That came within their view.

Now every old dogie with long flop ears,
  That didn't hole up by day,
Got his long ears trimmed and his old hide scorched,
  In the most artistic way.

Says Sandy Sam to Rusty Jiggs,
  As he threw his seago down:
"I figures I'm tired of cowpography,
  And I reckons I'll go to town."

So they saddled their ponies and struck a lope,
  For it was quite a ride,
But there was a place where an old cow-poke
  Could wet his dry inside.

Well, they started in at Kentucky Bar,
    Up at the head of the row,
And ended up at the Depot House,
    Just forty drinks below.

As they was a-comin' back to camp,
    A-carryin' the awful load,
Who should they meet but the Devil himself
    A-prancin' down the road.

Says the Devil to them: "Now, you cow-punchin' skunks,
    You'd better hunt your holes,
For I've come up from the rim rocks below
    To gather in your souls."

"The Devil be durned," says Sandy Sam,
    "Though I know that we are tight,
No Devil ever took an old cow-poke
    Without a regular fight."

So he built a hole in his old seago,
    And he threw it straight and true,
And he caught the Devil by both his horns,
    And he had it anchored, too.

Now, Rusty Jiggs was a reata man,
   With his gut line coiled up neat,
So he took it out and he built him a hole,
   And he snared the Devil's hind feet.

So they stretched him out and they tailed him down,
   And they got their irons red-hot,
And they put a swallow fork in each of his ears,
   And they scorched him up a lot.

Then they left him there in the Sierry Peaks
   Necked up to a big black oak,
Left him there in the Sierry Peaks,
   Tied knots in his tail for a joke.

Now, if you're ever up in the Sierry Peaks,
   And you hear an awful wail,
You'll know that it's the Devil himself,
   Crying 'bout the knots in his tail.

THE DRUNKARD'S LONE CHILD

I'm alone, all alone, my friends all have fled.

My father's a drunkard, my mother is dead.

I'm a poor little girl, I wander and weep

For the voice of my mother to sing me to sleep.

She sleeps on the hill in a bed made of clay.

How cold it did seem to lay mother away.

She's gone with the angels, and none do I see

So dear as the face of my mother to me.

'Tis springtime on earth, the birds seem so glad,
  I listen and wonder, my heart is so sad.
Sweet flowers bloom around, the crowd wanders by,
  But the form of my mother no longer is nigh.

Last night in my dreams she seemed to draw near.
  She pressed me as fondly as when she was here.
She smiled on me sweetly and fondled my brow
  And whispered: "Sleep on, I am watching thee now."

Refrain

I'm a little lone girl in this cold world so wild,
  God, look down and pity the drunkard's lone child.
Look down and pity. Oh, soon come to me,
  Take me to dwell with mother and Thee.

Here she comes, don't you hear the whistle blow?
　See the black smoke curling in the sky,
See the big head-light shining out so bright.
　Come out and watch her go by.

Hear that bell a-ringing, hear the darkies singing,
　Hold your hat on tight.
She's the 999 and if she's on time
　I'll see my baby tonight.

WAY DOWN YONDER IN THE CORN FIELD

Some folks say that a darky won't steal,
  'Way down yonder in the corn-field.
I caught two in my corn-field.
  'Way down yonder in the corn-field.

One had a shovel and the other had a hoe,
  'Way down yonder in the corn-field.
If this ain't stealing, I don't know.
  'Way down yonder in the corn-field.

One had a bushel and the other had a peck,
  'Way down yonder in the corn-field.
One had corn-stalk wrapped around his neck.
  'Way down yonder in the corn-field.

Mike Riley was a section boss,
    His shirts were made of scarlet floss.
He had a goat that did work hard
    To keep the weeds mown from his yard.

Now, Mike was courting widow Doan
    To spite a girl named Peggy Malone.
He washed his shirts and hung them high
    And left them there till night, to dry.

Of all the things this goat admired
    It was red shirts he most desired.
He gazed upon them thro the gate,
    He jumped the fence, those shirts he ate.

Mike came from work, both tired and sore.
    He missed his shirts and then he swore
He'd never seen the likes before,
    And, now, he'd have that old goat's gore.

He took the clothes-line from the yard
    And round that goat's neck tied it hard.
He placed a green light on its back
    And tied him on the rail-road track.

The train came fast with head-light bright,
    That poor goat shook and moaned with fright.
He gave one heave with might and main,
    Coughed up a shirt and flagged the train.

BECAUSE SHE AIN'T BUILT THAT WAY

Why is it a woman can't climb up a tree?
> Because she ain't built that way.
And why is it two of them never agree?
> Because they ain't built that way.
'Tis said that there is no effect without cause,
But a woman can never come under that clause,
For she never gives reason for wagging her jaws,
> Because she ain't built that way.

Don't give to your wife any secrets to keep,
> Because she ain't built that way.
For she couldn't hold them, not even in sleep
> Because she ain't built that way.
She'll keep you in water that's dreadfully hot
And she'll keep when she can all the change you have got.
But a secret, oh, Jiminy! certainly not,
> Because she ain't built that way.

Don't mash every girl that you see on the street,
> Because they ain't built that way.

376

Don't rave of her figure so perfect and neat,
> Because she ain't built that way.
With bustles and padding, and heels that are high,
> With blending of colors to capture the eye,
And the real from the sham you can't tell if you try
> Oh, there's lots of them built that way.

A woman cannot hit a barn with a stone,
> Because she ain't built that way.
And she can't bear to stay in a house all alone,
> Because she ain't built that way.
She can stay up all night at a masquerade ball
And tire every dancer there is in the hall.
Don't ask her to sew on a button, that's all,
> Because she ain't built that way.

A woman can never jump over a fence,
> Because she ain't built that way.
If a mad bull should chase her she has no defence,
> Because she ain't built that way.
She can kick up a row, upset every plan,
She's been noted for that since the world first began.
But she can't strike a match in the dark like a man
> Because she ain't built that way.

THE GYPSY'S WARNING

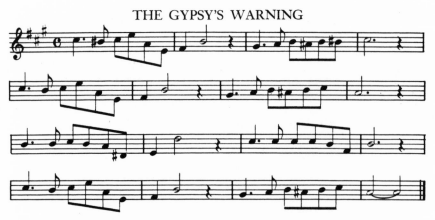

Trust him not, O gentle lady, though his voice be low and sweet.

Heed not him who kneels before thee softly pleading at thy feet.

Now thy life is in its morning; cloud not this thy happy lot.

Listen to the gipsy's warning — gentle lady, trust him not.

Lady, once there lived a maiden young and pure and like thee fair,

Yet he wooed, he wooed and won her, filled her gentle heart
with care.

Then he heeded not her weeping, he cared not her life to save!

Soon she perished; now she's sleeping in the cold and silent grave!

Lady, turn not from me coldly, what I say is only truth,

From a stern and withering sorrow, lady, I would shield thy
youth.

I would shield thee from all danger, shield thee from the tempter's
snare.

Lady, shun the dark-eyed stranger; I have warned thee, now
beware!

Take your gold, I do not want it; lady, I have prayed for this;

For the hour that I might foil him and rob him of expected bliss.

Aye, I see thou art filled with wonder at my looks so fierce and wild.

Lady, in the churchyard yonder, sleeps the gipsy's only child.

SWEET MARIE
(See also "Old-Fashioned Schottische" on page 162)

I've a secret in my heart, sweet Marie,

A tale I would impart, love, to thee.

Every daisy in the dell

Knows my secret, knows it well,

Yet to thee I dare not tell, sweet Marie.

When I hold your hand in mine, sweet Marie,

Then a feeling most divine comes to me.

All the world is full of spring,

Full of warblers on the wing,

And I listen while they sing, sweet Marie.

379

In the morn' when I awake, sweet Marie,
    Seems to me my heart will break, love, for thee.
Every wave that meets the shore
    Seems to sing it, o'er and o'er,
Seems to say that I adore, sweet Marie.

When the sunset tints the West, sweet Marie,
    And I sit down to rest, love, with thee.
Every star that studs the skies
    Seems to stand and wonder why,
They are dimmer than your eyes, sweet Marie.

Chorus

Come to me, sweet Marie,
    Sweet Marie, come to me.
Not because your face is fair, love, to see.
    But your soul so pure and sweet
Makes my happiness complete,
    Makes me falter at your feet, sweet Marie.

THE THINNEST MAN I EVER SAW

The thinnest man I ever saw
  Lived over in Hoboken,
And when I tell you how thin he was,
  You'll think I'm just a-joking.
He was thin as any postage stamp,
  Or the skin of a new potato.
For exercise he took a ride
  Through the holes of a nutmeg grater.

He never went out on a stormy night,
  He never went out alone,
For fear some poor old hungry dog
  Would take him for a bone.

He was sitting by the fire one night,
  The light was burning dimly,
When a bed-bug took him by the seat of the pants
  And yanked him up the chimney.

Chorus

1.   Oh me, oh my!
  He was the thinnest man.
As thin as the soup in a boarding house,
  Or the skin of a soft-shelled clam.

2.   Oh me, oh my!
  He almost lost his breath,
When he fell through a hole in the seat of his pants.
  And choked himself to death.

SHAMUS O'BRIEN

Oh, Shamus O'Brien, why don't you come home?
You don't know how happy I'd be.
I have but one wish and that you would come,
And forever be happy with me.

Chorus

Then fill up the glasses and drink what you like,
Whatever's the damage I'll pay.
Drink hearty and free while drinking with me,
For I'm a man you won't meet every day.

(See waltz on page 140)
(See also another version of "Shamus O'Brien" on page 405)

WHEN THE SWALLOWS HOMEWARD FLY

When the swallows homeward fly,
 When the roses scattered lie,
When from neither hill nor dale,
 Chants the silvery nightingale,
In these words my bleeding heart,
 Would to thee its grief impart,
When I thus thy image lose,
 Can I, ah, can I e'er know repose?
Can I, ah, can I e'er know repose?

When the white swan southward roves,
 To seek at noon the orange groves,
When the red tints of the West,
 Prove the sun has gone to rest,
In these words my bleeding heart,
 Would to thee its grief impart,
When I thus thy image lose,
 Can I, ah, can I e'er know repose?
Can I, ah, can I e'er know repose?

Hush, my heart! Why thus complain?
   Thou must, too, thy woes contain,
Tho' on earth no more we rove,
   Loudly breathing vows of love,
Thou, my heart, must find relief,
   Yielding to these words belief,
I shall see thy form again,
   Though today we part again,
Though today we part again.

OLD SAYINGS

As poor as a church mouse, as thin as a rail,
As fat as a porpoise, as slow as a snail,
As brave as a lion, as spry as a cat,
As bright as a sixpence, as weak as a rat,

As proud as a peacock, as sly as a fox,
As mad as a March hare, as strong as an ox,
As fair as a lily, as empty as air,
As rich as a Croesus, as cross as a bear.

As pure as an angel, as neat as a pin,
As smart as a steel-trap, as ugly as sin,
As dead as a door-nail, as white as a sheet,
As flat as a pan-cake, as red as a beet.

As round as an apple, as black as your hat,
As brown as a berry, as blind as a bat,
As mean as a miser, as full as a tick,
As plump as a partridge, as sharp as a stick.

As clean as a penny, as dark as a pall,
As hard as a mill-stone, as bitter as gall,
As fine as a fiddle, as clear as a bell,
As dry as a herring, as deep as a well.

As light as a feather, as hard as a rock,
As sharp as a needle, as calm as a clock,
As green as a gosling, as brisk as a bee,
And this is the end of the repertory.

386

SONG VERSES

OLD JOE CLARK

(Fiddle tune on page 121)

Old Joe Clark he had a barn,
It was sixteen stories high.
And every story in that barn
Was filled with chicken pie.

Old Joe Clark is dead and gone,
I hope he's doin' well.
He fed me on so many beans,
They made my belly swell.

Chorus

Sail around, Old Joe Clark.
Sail around the sea.
Sail around, Old Joe Clark.
I ain't got long to stay.

DRUNKEN SAILOR

(Fiddle tune on page 74)
(See "Old Brass Wagon" on page 248)
(See also "Old John Brown Had a Little Indian." on page 448)

What we goin' to do with the drunken sailor?
What we goin' to do with the drunken sailor?
What we goin' to do with the drunken sailor,
Before he starts another fight?

What's he goin' to do when he gets sober?
What's he goin' to do when he gets sober?
What's he goin' to do when he gets sober,
While he's in the brig for the night?

JORDAN AM A HARD ROAD TO TRABBEL

(Fiddle tune, "T'other Side of Jordan," on page 82)

I 'ribed into New York to pass de time away,
   I trabbl'd ober de Russ pav'ent accordin'.
Dey's gwine to hab it finish'd when de City Hall bell
   Sounds ober on de oder side ob Jordan.

Den I look to de Norf, and I look to de East,
   And I holler for de ox-cart to come on,
Wid four white horses a-driven on de lead,
   To take me to de odder side ob Jordan.

Den I clem in de hay-loft try'n to git asleep,
   Massa John went out to maul 'em.
He hit 'em on de head wid a cake ob soft soap,
   An' hit sounded on de odder side ob Jordan.

I went an' made a banjo, so well I keeps hit strung,
   An' 'range all my music accordin'.
I play 'em up a chune call'd "Sich a Gittin' Upstairs,"
   An' dey sing hit on de odder side ob Jordan.

Chorus

I took off my coat an' roll up my sleeve.
   Jordan am a hard road to trabbel.
I took off my coat an' roll up my sleeve.
   Jordan am a hard road to trabbel, I believe.

BUY A BROOM

(Tune, "Broom Waltz," on page 144)

From Deutchland I come with my light wares all laden,
  To the land where the blessing of freedom doth bloom.
Then listen, fair lady and young pretty maiden,
  Oh, buy of the wandering Bavarian a broom.

Chorus

Buy a broom, buy a broom.
Oh, buy of the wandering Bavarian a broom.

To brush away insects that sometimes annoy you,
  You'll find it quite handy to use night and day.
And what better exercise pray can employ you
  Than to sweep all vexatious intruders away?

Chorus

Buy a broom, buy a broom.
And sweep all vexatious intruders away.

Ere winter comes on, for sweet home soon departing,
  My toils for your favor again I'll resume.
And while gratitude's tear in my eyelid is starting,
  Bless the time that in England I cried, buy a broom.

Chorus

Buy a broom, buy a broom.
Bless the time that in England I cried, buy a broom.

Refrain

Ach du lieber Augustin, Augustin, Augustin.
Ach du lieber Augustin, alles ist hin.
s'Bier ist hin, d'Frau ist hin, alles mein Geld ist hin.
Ach du lieber Augustin, alles ist hin.

OLD ROSIN THE BEAU

(Tune "Rosin the Bow" on page 57)

I live for the good of my nation,
   And my sons are all growing low,
But I hope that my next generation
   Will resemble old Rosin the Beau.

I've traveled this country all over,
   And now to the next I will go,
For I know that good quarters await me,
   To welcome old Rosin the Beau.

In the gay round of pleasure I've traveled,
   Nor will I behind leave a foe;
And when my companions are jovial
   They will drink to old Rosin the Beau.

But my life is now drawn to a closing,
   As all will at last be so.
So we'll take a full bumper at parting,
   To the name of old Rosin the Beau.

When I'm dead and laid out on the counter,
   The people all making a show,
Just sprinkle plain whiskey and water,
   On the corpse of old Rosin the Beau.

I'll have to be buried, I reckon,
And the ladies will all want to know,
And they'll lift up the lid of my coffin,
Saying, "Here lies old Rosin the Beau."

Oh! when to my grave I am going,
The children will all want to go.
They'll run to the doors and the windows,
Saying, "There goes old Rosin the Beau."

Then pick me out six trusty fellows
And let them all stand in a row,
And dig a big hole in the meadow.
And in it toss Rosin the Beau.

Then bring out two little brown jugs,
Place one at my head and my toe,
And do not forget to scratch on them
The name of old Rosin the Beau.

Then let those trusty good fellows,
Oh! let them all stand in a row,
And turn up that big bellied bottle
And drink to old Rosin the Beau.

GREEN GROW THE RUSHES O!

(Fiddle tune on page 72)

There's naught but care on ev'ry han',
  In every hour that passes, O!
What signifies the life of man,
  An' 'twer na' for the lasses, O!

The warldly race may riches chase,
  An' riches still may fly them, O!
An' though at last they catch them fast,
  Their hearts can ne'er enjoy them, O!

Auld nature vows the lovely dears
  Her noblest works she classes, O!
Her 'prentice han' she tried on man,
  An' then she made the lasses, O!

Chorus

Green grow the rushes, O!
  Green grow the rushes, O!
The sweetest hours that e'er I've spent
  Were spent amang the lasses, O!

LUCY LONG

(Fiddle tune on page 59)

I jist come out afore you
  To sing a little song.
I plays it on the banjo
  And dey calls it Lucy Long.

Miss Lucy, she is han'some.
  Miss Lucy, she is tall.
To see her dance cachucha
  Would make de buildin's fall.

I ask her for to marry.
  She hadn't much to say.
But said she'd rather tarry,
  So I let her have her way,

My mammy's got de tisic.
  My daddy's got de gout.
Good morning, Mister phisick,
  Does your mother know you're out?

If I had a scolding wife,
  As sure as she was born,
I'd take her down to New Orleans
  And swop her off for corn.

Chorus

Oh, take your time, Miss Lucy.
  Take your time, Miss Lucy Long.
Oh, take your time, Miss Lucy.
  Take your time, Miss Lucy Long.

YANKEE DOODLE

(Children's play song "Yankee Doodle" on page 259)

Father and I went down to camp
  Along with Captain Goodin,
And there we saw the men and boys
  As thick as hasty puddin'.

And there was Captain Washington
  Upon a slapping stallion,
A-giving orders to his men,
  I guess there was a million.

And then the feathers on his hat,
  They looked so tarnal finey,
I wanted peskily to get
  To give to my Jemima.

And there they had a swamping gun,
  As big as a log of maple,
On a dinky little cart—
  A load for father's cattle.

And every time they fired it off
  It took a horn of powder.
It made a noise like father's gun,
  Only tarnation louder.

I went as near to it myself
  As Jacob's underpinnin',
And father went as near again—
  I thought the deuce was in him.

396

It scared me so, I ran ten miles,
  Nor stopped, as I remember,
Till I got home, and safely locked
  In granny's little chamber.

And then I see a little keg,
  Its heads were made of leather.
They knocked upon't with little sticks
  To call the folks together.

And there they fifed away like fun,
  And played on corn-stalk fiddles
And some had ribbons red as blood
  All bound around their middles.

The troopers, too, would gallop up
  And fire right in our faces.
It scared me almose half to death
  To see them run such races.

Uncle Sam came there to change
  Some pancakes and some onions,
For 'lasses cakes to carry home
  To give his wife and young'nes.

But I can't tell you half I see,   .
  They kept up such a bother.
So I took my hat off, made a bow
  And scampered home to mother.

DANCIN' ON DE GREEN

(Tune "Dancing in the Barn" on page 289)

Oh! way down in Souf Car'lina,
    Wheah de cotton an' de sugah cane grow,
It is funny 'mong de honey,
    For to see de niggers laugh an' crow!
We all gets up early in de mornin',
    An' to work we singin' all do go,
Always singin', voices ringin',
    Ah tells you were not slow.

Every month we do have a pahty,
    Whah de niggers an' dey ladies go;
Aunt Jemima, fum Car'lina,
    Comes along wif funny ol' Jim Crow.
Dar's ol' Josephus Orange Blossom,
    With his sweet gal Ann Eliza Jane,
Sister Mary, so contrary
    Had dancin' on de brain.

Chorus

Oh! we do have our fun, on a holiday we feel so gay.
    An' dis is what we do: (Break)
An' den we play on de banjo, de bones an' tambourine,
    In de mornin' or in de evenin', while dancin' on de green.

MOLLY, PUT THE KETTLE ON

(Fiddle tune on page 85)

Molly, put the kettle on, why don't you put the kettle on?
  Molly, put the kettle on, we'll all take tea.
Sukey, take it off again, why don't you take it off again?
  Sukey, take it off again, for they've all gone away.

Now put down the ginger cake, now put down the ginger cake.
  Stir the fire and let it bake, and we'll all take tea.
Put the muffins down to roast, put the muffins down to roast,
  Blow the fire and make the toast, and we'll all take tea.

Dolly, set the table out, Dolly set the table out,
  Move the dishes all about, and we'll all take tea.
Pass around the pumpkin pie, pass around the pumpkin pie
  And the fritters made of rye, and we'll all take tea.

T'OTHER SIDE OF JORDAN

(Fiddle tune on page 82)

I just arrived in town to pass the time away,
　And I settle all my business accordin',
But the weather turned so cold I heard a feller say:
　"I wish I was on 'tother side of Jordan."

I looked off to the East and I looked off to the West,
　And I see an old miser a-comin'
With his four bay horses hitched up to a chest,
　To tote his money to 'tother side of Jordan.

Oh, David and Goliath they both had a fight,
　And the Devil he came and slipped up behind them.
David hit Goliath with all his might,
　And it sounded on 'tother side of Jordan.

Chorus
Take off your coats, boys, and roll up our sleeves,
　For Jordan is a hard road to travel.
So take off your coats, boys, and roll up your sleeves,
　For Jordan is a hard road to travel.

OLD BOB RIDLEY
(Fiddle tune on page 54)

Oh listen, folks, I will sing you a ditty,
　I'm from home, but that's no pity.

To praise myself it is a shame,
 But old Bob Ridley is my name.

Oh listen, folks, I've just come from the mountain,
 How many miles I did not count 'em.
I left the folks on the old plantation,
 Come down here for my education.

The first time that I got a lickin'
 'Twas down in the field at the cotton pickin'.
It made me dance, and it made me tremble,
 And golly, it made my eye-balls jingle.

Chorus

I'm old Bob Ridley, Oh, I'm old Bob Ridley, Oh!
I'm old Bob Ridley, Oh, I'm old Bob Ridley, Oh!

TWINKLE, LITTLE STAR

(Fiddle tune on page 51)

The pretty little stars are laughing, love,
 The sky looks calm and clear.
The moon is shining brightly from above,
 'Tis time that you were here.
You said that you would surely come at eight,
 And with the twinkling stars,
Down by grandpa's meadow,
 You would meet me at the bars.

The pretty little stars are laughing, love,
 They speak to me of you.
They tell me as they twinkle up above,
 That you to me are true.
And the silvery moon peeping through the clouds,
 Behind the pretty stars,
Tells me 'tis eight and time that
 You should meet me at the bars.

SWEET EVELINA

(Tune on page 142)

Way down in the meadow, where the lily first blows,
  Where the wind from the mountain ne'er ruffles the rose,
Lives fond Evelina, the sweet little dove,
  The pride of the valley, the girl that I love.

She's fair as a rose, like a lamb she is meek,
  And she never was known to put paint on her cheek.
In the most graceful curls hangs her raven-black hair,
  And she never requires perfumery there.

Evelina and I, one evening in June,
  Took a walk all alone by the light of the moon.
The planets all shone, for the heavens were clear.
  And I felt round the heart, oh, most mightily queer.

Three years have gone by and I've not got a dollar.
  Evelina still lives in the green grassy hollow.
Although I am fated to marry her never,
  I'll love her, I'm sure, forever and ever.

Refrain

Sweet Evelina, dear Evelina,
My love for you shall never, never die.

403

JOHNNY MORGAN

(Fiddle tune on page 101)

I'll sing of a Band that used to play music in the street,
  And if you heard it you would say it was anything but sweet.
They all played different instruments, the music was the same.
  They were all one family, and Morgan was their name.

They used to say that Johnny was the smartest of them all,
  And round the area windows he would often make a call.
His music was so lively all the latest airs from France,
  The servant girls could not keep still, the music made them dance.

Now one day John he chanced to play outside a lady's door,
  And the lady said she'd never heard such music played before.
It pleased her so that you must know, she heavy sums would pay
  To John, to stand outside the house and play to her all day.

Chorus
Johnny Morgan played the organ, the father beat the drum.
  The sister played the tambourine, the brother went pom, pom,
                            pom, — pom, pom, pom.
All alone on an old trombone, the music was so sweet,
  They often got a penny to go into another street.

SHAMUS O'BRIEN

(Tune on page 140)

Oh! sweet is the smile of the beautiful morn
  As it peeps through the curtain of night,
And the voice of the nightingale singing his tune
  While the stars seem to smile with delight.

All nature now lingers in silent repose
  And the breath of sweet summer in calm,
While I sit and wonder if Shamus e'er knows
  How sad and unhappy I am!

Chorus

Oh! Shamus O'Brien why don't you come home?
  You don't know how happy I'll be;
I've one darling wish, it's that you would come
  And forever be happy with me!

I'll smile when you smile and I'll weep when you weep
  I'll give you a kiss for a kiss,
And all the fond vows that I've made you I'll keep.
  What more can I promise than this?

Does the sea have such bright and such beautiful charms
  That your heart will not leave it for me?
Oh! why did I let you go out of my arms
  Like a bird that was caged and is free?

405

Chorus

Oh! Shamus O'Brien, I'm loving you yet,
    And my heart is still trusting and kind.
It was you who first took it, and can you forget,
    That love for another you'd find?

No! No! if you break it with sorrow and pain
    I'll then have a duty to do;
If you'll bring it to me, I'll mend it again,
    And trust it, dear Shamus, to you.

CLEAR THE KITCHEN

(Fiddle tune on page 105)

In old Kantuck in the arternoon,
  We sweep the floor with a bran' new broom,
And arter that we form a ring,
  And this is the song that we do sing, O!

I went to the creek, I couldn't get across,
  I'd nobody with me but an old blind hoss.
But old Jim Crow come a-ridin' by,
  Sez he: "Old feller, your hoss will die."

My hoss fell down upon the spot,
  Sez he: "Don't ye see his eyes is sot?"
So I took my knife and off with his skin,
  And if he comes to life I'll ride him agin.

A jay-bird sot on a hickory limb,
  He winked at me and I winked at him.
I picked up a rock and I hit his shin,
  Sez he: "You'd better not do that agin."

A bull-frog dressed in soldier's clothes,
  Went out in the field to shoot some crows.
The crows smell powder and fly away,
  That bull-frog mighty mad that day.

407

Chorus

Clear the kitchen, old folks, young folks,
Clear the kitchen, old folks, young folks,
Old Virginny never tire.

A LIFE ON THE OCEAN WAVE

(Fiddle tune on page 33)

A life on the ocean wave,
  A home on the rolling deep,
Where the scattered waters rave,
  And the winds their revels keep!
Like an eagle caged, I pine
  On this dull unchanging shore.
Oh, give me the flashing brine,
  The spray and the tempest's roar!
Once more on the deck I stand,
  Of my own swift gliding craft.
Set sail! Farewell to the land,
  The gale follows far abaft.
We shoot through the sparkling foam,
  Like an ocean bird set free,
Like the ocean birds, our home
  We'll find far out on the sea!

Refrain

A life on the ocean wave,
    A home on the rolling deep!
Where the scattered waters rave,
    And the winds their revels keep!

BUFFALO GIRLS
(Fiddle tune on page 53)

As I was walking down the street,
    Down the street, down the street,
A pretty little girl I chanced to meet,
    Oh, she was fair to see.

I asked her if she would have some talk,
    Have some talk, have some talk.
Her feet covered up the whole sidewalk,
    As she stood close to me.

I asked her would she have a dance,
    Have a dance, have a dance.
I thought that I might get a chance
    To shake a foot with her.

I'd like to make that gal my wife,
  Gal my wife, gal my wife.
I would be happy all my life,
  If I had her by my side.

Chorus

Buffalo gals, ain't you comin' out tonight,
  Ain't you comin' out tonight, ain't you comin' out tonight,
Buffalo gals, ain't you comin' out tonight,
  And dance by the light of the moon.

DEM GOLDEN SLIPPERS

(Fiddle tune on page 113)

Oh, my golden slippers am laid away,
  'Kase I don't 'spect to wear 'em till my weddin' day,
An' my long-tailed coat, dat I love so well,
  I will wear up in de chariot in de morn.

An' my long white robe dat I bo't las' June,
  I'se gwine to git chang'd 'kase it fits too soon,
An' de old gray hoss dat I used to drive,
  I will hitch 'im to de chariot in de morn.

Oh, my ol' banjo hangs on de wall,
  'Kase it ain't been tuned since 'way las' fall.
But de darkies all say we'll hab a good time,
  When we ride up in de chariot in de morn.

Dar's brudder Ben and sister Luce,
  Dey'll telegraph de news to uncle 'Backer Juice.

What a great camp meetin' dar will be dat day,
   When ye ride up in der chariot in de morn.

So it's good-bye, chillun, I have for to go,
   Whar de rain don't fall or de wind don't blow,
An' yer ulster coats, why, ye will not need,
   When ye ride up in de chariot in de morn.

But yer golden slippers must be nice and clean,
   An' yer age must be just sweet sixteen,
An' yer white kid gloves ye'll have to wear,
   When ye ride up in de chariot in de morn.

Chorus

Oh, dem golden slippers! Oh, dem golden slippers!
Golden slippers I'se gwine to wear, 'kase dey look so neat.
Oh, dem golden slippers! Oh, dem golden slippers!
Golden slippers I'se gwine to wear, to walk de golden street!

POP GOES THE WEASEL
(Fiddle tune on page 40)

All around the meetin' house,
   The monkey chased the weasel,
Every time the monkey jumps,
   Pop goes the weasel.

A penny for a spool of thread,
   A penny for a needle.

That's the way the money goes,
 Pop goes the weasel.

Rufus has the whooping cough,
 Sally has the measles.
That's the way the doctor goes,
 Pop goes the weasel.

OLD DAN TUCKER

(Tune on page 55)

I went down to town the other night,
 I heard a noise and I saw a fight.
The watchman he was runnin' round,
 Cryin': "Old Dan Tucker's come to town."

Old Dan Tucker went down to the mill,
 To get some meal to put in the swill,
The miller swore by the point of his knife,
 That he never seen such a man in his life.

Old Dan Tucker he got drunk,
 And he fell in the fire and he kicked up a chunk.
A red-hot coal rolled in his shoe,
 And good lawsy, massa, how the ashes flew.

Old Dan Tucker was a fine old man,
 But he washed his face in the frying-pan.

He combed his hair with a wagon wheel,
And he died with the toothache in his heel.

Chorus

Get out of the way for old Dan Tucker,
Get out of the way for old Dan Tucker,
Get out of the way for old Dan Tucker,
He come too late to get his supper.

OLD ZIP COON

(Tune Turkey in the Straw on page 59)

I went down to Sandy Hook the other afternoon,
I went down to Sandy Hook the other afternoon,
I went down to Sandy Hook the other afternoon;
And the first man I met there was old Zip Coon.

Old Zip Coon is a very fine scholar,
Old Zip Coon is a very fine scholar,
Old Zip Coon is a very fine scholar,
And he plays upon the banjo "Coonie in the Hollow."

Old Sukey Blueskin fell in love with me,
Old Sukey Blueskin fell in love with me,
Old Sukey Blueskin fell in love with me,
She invited me home to take a cup of tea.

What do you think old Sukey had for supper?
What do you think old Sukey had for supper?

What do you think old Sukey had for supper?
Chicken foot, spar grass and apple sauce butter.

I'LL BE ALL SMILES TONIGHT

(Tune on page 137)

I'll deck my brow with roses,
  The loved one will be there.
The gems that others gave me
  Will shine within my hair.
And even them that know me,
  Will think my heart is light,
Though my heart may break tomorrow,
  I'll be all smiles tonight!

And when the room he entered,
  The bride upon his arm.
I stood and gazed upon him
  As if he was a charm.
So now he smiles upon her,
  So once he smiled on me,
They know not what I've suffered,
  They found no change in me.

And when the dance commences,
  Oh, how I will rejoice!
I'll sing the song he taught me,
  Without a faltering voice.

414

When the flatterers come around me,
  They will think my heart is light,
Though my heart will break tomorrow,
  I'll be all smiles tonight.

And when the dance is over,
  And all have gone to rest,
I'll think of him, dear mother,
  The one that I love best.
He once did love me, believe me,
  But now has grown cold and strange,
He sought not to deceive me,
  False friends have wrought this change.

Chorus

I'll be all smiles tonight, love,
  I'll be all smiles tonight.
Though my heart may break tomorrow,
  I'll be all smiles tonight.

LITTLE BROWN JUG

(Fiddle tune on page 33)

My wife and I lived all alone,
  In a little log hut we called our own.
She loved gin and I loved rum,
  I tell you what, we'd lots of fun.

'Tis you who make my friends my foes,
  'Tis you who make me wear old clothes.
Here you are so near my nose,
  So tip her up and down she goes.

When I go toiling to my farm,
  I take little brown jug under my arm.
I place it under a shady tree,
  Little brown jug, 'tis you and me.

If all the folks in Adam's race,
  Were gathered together in one place.
Then I'd prepare to shed a tear,
  Before I part with you, my dear.

If I had a cow that gave such milk,
  I'd clothe her in the finest silk.
I'd feed her on the choicest hay,
  And milk her forty times a day.

The rose is red, my nose is too,
  The violet's blue and so are you.
And yet, I guess, before I stop
  We'd better take another drop.

Chorus

Ha! Ha! Ha! you and me,
  Little brown jug, don't I love thee!

Ha! Ha! Ha! you and me,
Little brown jug, don't I love thee!

THE GIRL I LEFT BEHIND ME

(Fiddle tune on page 116)

I'm lonesome since I crossed the hill,
And o'er the moor and valley.
Such heavy thoughts my heart do fill,
Since parting with my Sally.

I seek no more the fine and gay,
For each does but remind me,
How swift the hours did pass away,
With the girl I left behind me.

Oh, never shall I forget that night,
The stars were bright above me,
And gently lent their silvery light,
When first she vowed she loved me.

But now I'm bound to Brighton camp,
Kind heaven, may favor find me,
And send me safely back again,
To the girl I left behind me.

417

The bee shall honey taste no more,
   The dove become a ranger.
The dashing waves shall cease to roar
   Ere she's to me a stranger.

The vows we've registered above
   Shall ever cheer and bind me
In constancy to her I love,
   The girl I left behind me.

My mind her form shall still retain,
   In sleeping or in waking.
Until I see my love again,
   For whom my heart is breaking.

If ever I should see the day
   When Mars shall have resigned me,
For evermore I'l gladly stay
   With the girl I left behind me.

KEMO KIMO

(Fiddle tune on page 106)

In South Car'lina de darkies go
   Sing song, Kitty, can't you ki'me, O!

Dat's whar de white folks plant de tow,
　Sing song, Kitty, can't you ki'me, O!

Cover de ground all over wid smoke,
　Sing song, Kitty, can't you ki'me, O!
And up de darkies heads dey poke.
　Sing song, Kitty, can't you ki'me, O!

Dar was a frog lived in a pool,
　Sing song, Kitty, can't you ki'me, O!
Sure he was de biggest fool,
　Sing song, Kitty, can't you ki'me, O!

But he could dance and he could sing.
　Sing song, Kitty, can't you ki'me, O!
And make de woods around him ring,
　Sing song, Kitty, can't you ki'me, O!

Chorus

Kemo, Kimo! Dar! Oh, whar?
　Wid my hi, my ho, and in come Sally, singing.
Sometimes penny-winkle-lingtum, nip-cat.
　Sing song, Kitty, can't you ki'me, O!

SALLY GOODIN'
(Fiddle tune on page 64)

I had a piece a' pie,
　And I had a piece a' puddin',
And I gave it all away,
　For to see Sally Goodin'.

A sheep and a cow,
  A-walkin' in the pasture.
The sheep said: "Cow,
  Can't you walk a little faster?"

I went to the river,
  And the river was up.
Along came a coon,
  And a yaller houn' pup.

You had a piece a' pie,
  And you had a piece a' puddin',
Now, don't you forget,
  For to swing Sally Goodin!

Swing grandma! Swing grandpa!
  Swing that gal from Arkansaw!
Come on, boys, don't be afraid!
  Swing Sally Goodin' and all promenade!

POLLY WOLLY DOODLE
(Fiddle tune on page 66)

Oh, I went down South for to see me Sal,
  Sing Polly Wolly Doodle all the day.
My Sally is a spunky gal,
  Sing Polly Wolly Doodle all the day.

Oh, my Sal she is a maiden fair,
  Sing Polly Wolly Doodle all the day.

With curly eyes and laughing hair,
  Sing Polly Wolly Doodle all the day.

Oh, a grasshopper sittin' on a railroad track,
  Sing Polly Wolly Doodle all the day.
A-pickin' his teeth with a carpet tack,
  Sing Polly Wolly Doodle all the day.

Oh, I went to bed, but it wasn't no use,
  Sing Polly Wolly Doodle all the day.
My feet stuck out like a chicken roost,
  Sing Polly Wolly Doodle all the day.

Behind the barn down on my knees,
  Sing Polly Wolly Doodle all the day.
I thought I heard a chicken sneeze,
  Sing Polly Wolly Doodle all the day.

He sneezed so hard with the whooping cough,
  Sing Polly Wolly Doodle all the day.
He sneezed his head and tail right off,
  Sing Polly Wolly Doodle all the day.

Chorus

Fare thee well, fare thee well,
  Fare thee well, my fairy fay.
For I'm goin' to Louisiana, for to see my Susyanna,
  Sing Polly Wolly Doodle all the day.

WAIT FOR THE WAGON

(Fiddle tune on page 119)

Will you come with me, my Phillis dear,
  To yon blue mountain free.
Where the blossoms smell the sweetest —
  Come, rove along with me.

It's every Sunday morning,
  When I am by your side.
We'll jump into the wagon,
  And all take a ride.

Where the river runs like silver,
  And the birds they sing so sweet.
I have a cabin, Phillis,
  And something good to eat.

Come, listen to my story,
  It will relieve my heart,
So jump into the wagon,
  And off we will start.

Chorus

Wait for the wagon, wait for the wagon,
Wait for the wagon and we'll all take a ride.

CAPTAIN JINKS

(Fiddle tune on page 120)

(See also "Down the Ohio" on page 242)

I'm Captain Jinks, of the Horse Marines,
   I feed my horse on corn and beans,
And sport young ladies in their teens,
   Though a captain in the Army.
I teach young ladies how to dance,
   How to dance, how to dance,
I teach young ladies how to dance,
   For I'm the pet of the army.

I joined my corps when twenty-one,
   Of course I thought it capital fun.
When the enemy came, of course I run,
   For I'm not cut out for the Army,
When I left home, mamma she cried,
   Mamma she cried, mamma she cried,
When I left home mamma she cried:
   "He's not cut out for the Army."

Chorus
I'm Captain Jinks of the Horse Marines,
   I feed my horse on corn and beans,
And often live beyond my means,
   Tho' a captain in the army.

ROOT, HOG, OR DIE

(Fiddle tune on page 60)

I'm right from old Virginia, with my pocket full of news,
  I'm worth twenty shillings, right square in my shoes.
It doesn't make a bit of difference to neither you or I,
  Big pig, or little pig, it's root, hog, or die.

Now I'm the happiest bozo on the top of the earth,
  And I get fat as a 'possum in the time of the dearth.
Like a pig in a 'tater patch, there let me lie,
  'Way out in Kansas where it's root, hog, or die.

Chorus
  I'm chief cook and bottle washer,
    Captain of the waiters.
  I stand upon my head,
    When I peel them scrawny 'taters.

JIM CROW

(Fiddle tune on page 83)

Come listen, all you gals and boys,
  I'm just from Tuckyhoe.
I'm goin' to sing a little song,
  My name's Jim Crow.

I went down to the river,
  I didn't mean to stay.
But there I saw so many gals,
  I couldn't get away.

And arter I'd been there awhile,
  I thought I'd push my boat.
But I tumbled in the river,
  And find myself afloat.

I git upon a flat boat,
  I ketch the Uncle Sam.
Then I went to see the place where
  They killed the Packenham.

And then I got to Orleans,
  And feel so full of fight.
They put me in the calaboose,
  And keep me there all night.

When I got out I hit a man,
  His name I now forgot,
But there was nothing left of him,
  'Cept a little greasy spot.

Chorus
Wheel about and turn about and do jis' so.
Every time I wheel about I jump Jim Crow.

PARODIES

These verses have been sung by funmakers in every walk of life. Most of them originated in a space of time ranging from the Civil War to about 1900.

THE SONG OF STATES
(Tune: "It Ain't Goin to Rain No More")

Oh, what did Tennessee, boys?
  Oh, what did Tennessee?
Oh, what did Tennessee, boys?
  Oh, what did Tennessee?

Oh, what did Tennessee, boys?
  Oh, what did Tennessee?
I ask you again, as a personal friend,
  What did Tennessee?

She saw what Arkansaw, boys,
  I tell you again.
Oh, where has Oregon, boys?
  She's taking Oklahome.

Oh, how did Wisconsin, boys?
  She stole a Newbrass-key.
Oh, what did Connecti-cut, boys?
  She cut Mississip-pi.

Oh, what did Dela-ware, boys?
  She wore a New Jersey.
Oh, where did Ida-ho, boys?
  She hoed in Maryland.

Oh, what did Io-wa, boys?
  She weighed a Washing-ton.
Oh, what made Chicago ill, boys?
  Too much Illinois.

Why does Baton Rouge, boys?
  If you'll wait, Al-ask-a.
What does Jamaica make, boys?
  She makes Virginia gin.

SONG OF SONG TITLES
(Tune: "It Aint Goin' to Rain no More")

Kind friends, listen for a while,
  I won't detain you long.
I'll tell you of some titles
  Of some very ancient songs.

Old Micky Brannigan had a bull pup,
  Way Down Where the Pansies Grow.
Don't Leave your Dear Old Mother, Tom,
  For Mary Kelly's Beau.

I'll tie White Wings with a Peek-a-Boo,
  With a knot of Blue and Grey.
I'll get The Letter that Never Came,
  On St. Patrick's Day.

I'll ride Paddy's cart,
   To Dear Old Ireland,
Where they play Yankee-doodle,
   In The Little German Band.

The Girl I Left Behind Me,
   Will love me once again,
When the Leaves Begin to Turn,
   Good-bye, Liza Jane.

I stole the Harp from Tara's Hall,
   While Waiting in the Rain.
I'll Take you Home Again, Kathleen,
   When The Robin Nests Again.

I'll show you How Paddy Stole the Rope,
   From babies in our block.
I owe ten dollars to Old D. Grady,
   On Grandfather's Clock.

She said I was A Warrior Bold,
   The day I played baseball.
I knew she'd Call Me Back Again,
   From Over the Garden Wall.

Them Golden Slippers I laid away,
  They fit Barney McCoy.
I'll present The Flowers that Bloom in the Spring,
  To Papa's Baby Boy.

Good-bye, My Honey, I'm Gone,
  Down at the Garden Gate.
Roasting Chestnuts By the Fire,
  The hour is getting late.

I had Fifteen Dollars in My Inside Pocket,
  I've Never Done Anything Since.
I'll Meet Her When the Sun goes Down,
  If I had But Fifteen Cents.

Norene, Morene and Sally Green,
  And Little Widow Dunn,
Are all alone in their Home, Sweet Home,
  Johnny, Get your Gun.

PADDY'S CURIOSITY SHOP
(Tune "Rosin the Bow" on page 57)

Don't talk about Barnum's Museum,
  For in passing my house you may stop.
There's things you'll be struck for to see 'em,
  In Paddy's Curiosity Shop.

I've all sorts of relics and stones,
   I've patch coats without any stitches.
I've some of Calverie's bones,
   And a pair of King David's old breeches.

I've the tree that lump sugar grows on,
   Without being damaged or hurt.
I've the handkerchief Moll blew his nose on,
   And Queen Elizabeth's Balmoral shirt.

I've old Mother Hubbard's chicken-coop,
   And old Mother Chicket's birch broom.
The one the old gal flew astride of
   When she dined with the man in the moon.

I've a walking stick that's not very pliant,
   In fact, it's not very strong.
It belonged to a famed Irish giant,
   Just two and thirty foot long.

His boots, too, they were like towers,
   A colt inside them you could drive,
If you should fall in them — Och, by the powers!
   You'd never be got out alive.

MARCHING ON GEORGIA
(Tune: "Marching Through Georgia")

Georgia was a little girl who lived in Tennessee,
　She had a ticklish feeling on her ankle and her knee.
Upon investigation, found a chigger and a flea,
　Hot dog! They were marching on Georgia!

Chorus
"Hurrah! Hurree!" said the chigger to the flea,
　"Hooray! Hurree!" said the chigger to the flea.
"You bite her on the ankle and I'll bite her on the knee,
　And, boy, we'll go marching on Georgia."

THE MULE
(Tune "Auld Lang Syne" on page 44)

On mules we find two legs behind,
　And two we find before.
We stand behind before we find
　What the two behind be for.
So stand before the two behind,
　And behind the two before.

FATHER'S WHISKERS
(Tune "The Parlor," on page 296)

I have a dear old father,
　For whom I nightly pray.

He has a bunch of whiskers,
   They're always in the way.

At supper in the evening,
   Around the family group,
My dear old father's whiskers
   Get tangled in the soup.

My dear old mother chews them
   At night when she's asleep,
And dreams that she is eating
   A bowl of shredded wheat.

Chorus

They're always in the way,
   The cows chew them for hay.
They hide the dirt on father's shirt,
   They're always in the way.

TURKEY IN THE STRAW
(Tune on page 59)

As I went down the new-cut road,
   I met Miss Possum and I met Mr. Toad.
And every time the toad would sing,
   The possum cut the pigeon-wing.

435

Turkey in the straw, haw! haw! haw!

 Turkey in the hay, hey! hey! hey!

The bull-frog danced with his mother-in-law,

 And they played 'em up a tune called turkey in the straw.

WE'LL ALL PULL THROUGH

(Tune "Turkey in the Straw" on page 59)

Oh, the mule's gone lame, the hens won't lay,

 Corn's way down, wheat don't pay.

Hog's no better, steer's too cheap,

 Cow's quit milkin', meat won't keep.

Oats all heated, spuds all froze,

 Wheat crop's busted, wind still blows.

Looks some gloomy, I'll admit.

 Git up, Dobbin! We ain't down yit.

Oh, the coal's too high, crops too low,

 Freight rates doubled, got no show.

Money's tighter, morals loose.

 Bound to get us. What's the use?

Sun's not shinin' as it should,

 Moon ain't beamin' like it could.

No use stoppin' to debate,

 Git up, Dobbin! It's gittin' late.

Oh, the wheels all wobble, the axle's bent,
　　Dashboard's broken, top all rent.
One shaft's splintered, t'other sags,
　　Seat's all busted, end-gate drags.

May hang together, b'lieve it will,
　　Careful drivin'll make it still.
Road's smoothed out till it won't seem true.
　　Git up, Dobbin! We'll pull through.

THE DUMMY LINE
(Tune "Turkey in the Straw" on page 59)

Across the prairie on a streak of rust,
　　There's something moving in a cloud of dust.
It crawls into the village with a wheeze and whine,
　　It's the two o'clock flyer on the dummy line.

I saw a snail go whizzing past.
　　A guy said: "My, this train is fast."
Said I: "Old man, that may be true,
　　But the question is, what's it fastened to?"

I said to the brakeman: "Can't you speed up a bit?"
　　Said he: "You can walk if you don't like it."
Said I: "Old man, I'd take your dare,
　　But the folks don't expect me till the train gets there."

437

Chorus

Ridin' on the dummy, on the dummy line,
  Rain or shine I'll pay my fine,
Rain or shine I'll pay my fine,
  Ridin' on the dummy, on the dummy line.

TOUGH LUCK
(Tune "Turkey in the Straw" on page 59)

Oh, his horse went dead, and his mule went lame,
  And he lost six cows. What a measly shame!
Then a hurricane came on a summer's day
  And blew the house where he lived away.

An earthquake came when this was gone
  And swallowed up the land that the house stood on.
Then the tax collector came around,
  And charged him up with a hole in the ground.

THE TRAIN PULLED IN THE STATION
(Tune "Wearing of the Green" on page 114)

Oh, the train pulled in the station,
  The bell was ringing wet.
The track ran by the depot
  And I think it's running yet.

Oh, I jumped into the river,
  Just because it had a bed.

438

I took a sheet of water,
  For to cover up my head.

'Twas midnight on the ocean,
  Not a street car was in sight.
While the sun and moon were shining,
  And it rained all day that night.

'Twas a summer day in winter,
  And the snow was raining fast,
As a barefoot boy, with shoes on,
  Stood sitting in the grass.

CONUNDRUM SONG
(Tune "Wearing of the Green" on page 114)

Do ships have eyes when they go to sea?
  Are there springs in the ocean bed?
Does the jolly tar flow from a tree?
  Does a river ever lose its head?
Are fishes crazy when they go in seine?
  Can an old hen sing her lay?
Can you give relief to a windowpane?
  Can you mend the break of day?
What vegetable is a policeman's beat?
  Is a newspaper white when it's read?
Is a baker broke when he's making dough?
  Is an undertaker's business dead?

439

Would a wall-paper store make a good hotel,
   On account of the borders there?
Would you paint a rabbit on a bald man's head,
   Just to give him a little hair?

THERE WAS A LITTLE HEN
(Tune "Old Soldier" on page 38)

Oh, there was a little hen,
   And she had a wooden foot,
And she laid her eggs
   In the mulberry root.
She laid more eggs
   Than any hen on the farm.
Another little drink
   Wouldn't do us any harm.

Chorus

Save up your money,
   And save up your chalk,
And you'll always have tobacco
   In your old tobacco box.

WHOA, MULE, WHOA!
(Tune on page 295)

I went to see Miss Liza Jane,
   To take her for a ride.
My ol' mule was so frisky,
   He'd run awhile, then slide.

440

Whoa, mule, whoa!
Whoa, mule, I say!
Just hop right in, Miss Liza,
And hold on to the sleigh.

We went down through old Tucker's lane,
   The neighbor's they did stare.
I wanted to kiss Liza,
   But I couldn't do it there.

Chorus

Whoa, mule, whoa!
You could hear them holler:
"Better tie a knot in that mule's tail,
Or he'll jump right through the collar."

I took Miss Liza to the parson's,
   Miss Liza, you keep cool.
I sho' would like to kiss you,
   But I'se busy with this mule.

Chorus

Whoa, mule, whoa!
Whoa, mule, I say!
If you get out, Miss Liza Jane,
It'll be our weddin' day.

BOUGHT A ROOSTER

(Tune "Goodbye, My Lover, Goodbye" on page 304)

Bought a rooster for fifteen cents,
Good-bye, my lover, good-bye.
The little devil, he jumped the fence.
Good-bye, my lover, good-bye.

I asked my mother for fifteen cents,
Good-bye, my lover, good-bye.
To see the elephant jump the fence,
Good-bye, my lover, good-bye.

Chorus

Bye-O, my rooster, he'll never crow like he uster,
Bye-O, my rooster, good-bye, my money, good-bye.

PUPIL'S SONG

(Tune "The Rye Waltz" on page 137)

If a body find a lesson rather hard and dry,
    If no body comes to show him, need a body cry?
If he's little time to study, should he stop and sigh?
    E'er he says, "I can not learn it," ought he not to try?

If a body scan his lesson with a steady eye,
    All its hardness he will conquer, conquer by and by.
Then how nicely he'll repeat it, face not all awry,
    Ne'er again he'll say he can not, but will go and try.

POP, GOES THE QUESTION

(Tune "Pop, Goes the Weasel" on page 40)

List to me, sweet maiden pray.
  Pop, goes the question!
Will you marry me, yea, or nay?
  Pop, goes the question!
I've no time to plead or sigh,
No patience to wait for by-and-by.
Snare me now, or I'm sure to fly.
  Pop, goes the question!

Ask papa, Oh! fiddle-de-dee.
  Pop, goes the question!
Fathers and lovers ne'er agree.
  Pop, goes the question!
He can't tell what I want to know,
Whether you love, sweet, or no;
To ask him, that would be very slow.
  Pop, goes the question!

I think we'd make such a charming pair.

    Pop, goes the question!

For I'm good-looking and you're very fair.

    Pop, goes the question!

We'll travel life's round in gallant style,

And you shall drive every other mile,

Or, if it please you all the while.

    Pop, goes the question!

If we don't have an enchanting time,

    Pop, goes the question!

I'm sure it will be no fault of mine.

    Pop, goes the question!

To be sure my funds make a feeble show,

But love is nourishing food, you know,

And cottage rent uncommonly low.

    Pop, goes the question!

Then answer me quickly, darling, pray.

    Pop, goes the question!

Will you marry me, yea, or nay?

    Pop, goes the question!

I've no time to plead or sigh,

No patience to wait for by-and-by.

Snare me now, or I'm sure to fly.

    Pop, goes the question!

445

UNCLE SAM'S FARM

(Tune "History of the World" on page 278)

Of all the mighty nations in the East or in the West,
  O, this glorious Yankee nation is the greatest and the best.
We have room for all creation and our banner is unfurled.
  Here's a general invitation to the people of the world.

St. Lawrence marks our Northern line as fast her waters flow,
  And the Rio Grande our Southern bound, way down to Mexico.
From the great Atlantic Ocean where the sun begins to dawn,
  Leap across the Rocky mountains, far away to Oregon.

While the South shall raise the cotton and the West the corn and
  New England manufactories shall do up the finer work.   [pork,
For the deep and flowing waterfalls that course along our hills,
  Are just the thing for washing sheep and driving cotton mills.

Our fathers gave us Liberty, but little did they dream,
  The grand results that pour along this mighty age of steam.
For our mountains, lakes and rivers, are all a blaze of fire,
  And we send our news by lightning on the telegraphic wire.

Yes! we're bound to beat the nations, for our motto's "Go ahead,"
  And we'll tell the foreign gentry that our people are well fed.
For the nations must remember Uncle Sam is not a fool,
  For the people do the voting and the children go to school.

Chorus

Then come along, come along, make no delay.
  Come from every nation, come from every way.
Our lands, they are broad enough, don't be alarmed,
  For Uncle Sam is rich enough to give us all a farm.

446

HOOPS, MY DEARS!

(Tune "T'other Side of Jordan" on page 82)

As hoops are all the rage now, you mustn't think it strange,
    If I say a few words all about them.
For the safety of our race I should like to see a change.
    Why can't the ladies get along without them?

They say the other day that a lady on the street
    Had hoops of such very large dimension,
That they suddenly burst, threw some gents off their feet.
    "Oh," they cried, "What a horrible invention!"

One cold blustering day when the wind blew very high
    A lady thought she'd venture out a-walking.
A sudden gust took her — you'd a laughed to've seen her fly!
    It was funny! Oh, there's no use a-talking!

Since the good days of Eve, Oh, it is very true
    That ladies all have ever been good-looking.
And I think it rather queer, now, ladies dear, that you
    Can't get along without such a-hooping!

Oh, ladies, please excuse me and do not take offence
    At what I have seen fit to mention.
Don't come with a "cooper shop" in self defence,
    Or denounce me at a "woman's right" convention.

447

OLD JOHN BROWN HAD A LITTLE INDIAN

(Fiddle tune, "Drunken Sailor," on page 74)

(See "Old Brass Wagon" on page 248)

(See Song verses "Drunken Sailor" on page 389)

Old John Brown had a little Indian,
　Old John Brown had a little Indian,
Old John Brown had a little Indian,
　One little Indian boy.

One little, two little, three little Indians,
　Four little, five little, six little Indians,
Seven little, eight little, nine little Indians,
　Ten little Indian boys.

Ten little, nine little, eight little Indians,
　Seven litrle, six little, five little Indians,
Four little, three little, two little Indians,
　One little Indian boy.

THREE CROWS

(Tune "When Johnny Comes Marching Home" on page 322)

There were three crows sat on a tree,
   O Billy McGee, O Billy McGee;
And they were black as crows could be,
   O Billy McGee, McGaw.
And they all flapped their wings and cried:
   (*Spoken*: Caw! Caw! Caw! Caw!) Billy McGee, McGaw.

Said one old crow unto his mate:
   "O Billy McGee, O Billy McGee,
What shall we do for grub to eat?
   O Billy McGee, McGaw."
And they all flapped their wings and cried:
   (Caw! Caw! Caw! Caw!) Billy McGee, McGaw.

"There lies a horse on yonder plain,
   O Billy McGee, O Billy McGee,
Who's by some cruel butcher slain,
   O Billy McGee, McGaw."
And they all flapped their wings and cried:
   (Caw! Caw! Caw! Caw!) Billy McGee, McGaw.

"We'll perch upon his bare back-bone
   O Billy McGee, O Billy McGee,
And pick his eyes out, one by one,
   O Billy McGee, McGaw."
And they all flapped their wings and cried:
   (Caw! Caw! Caw! Caw!) Billy McGee, McGaw.

449

POLLY KIMO

(Fiddle tune "Kemo Kimo" on page 106)

In South Carolina de niggers grow,
   Sing song, Polly, won't you ki' me, oh?
If de white man only plant his toe,
   Sing song, Polly, won't you ki' me, oh?
Water de ground with 'bacca smoke,
   Sing song, Polly, won't you ki' me, oh?
And up de nigger's head will poke,
   Sing song, Polly, won't you ki' me, oh?

Way down South in Cedar street,
   Sing song, Polly, won't you ki' me, oh?
Dar's whar de niggers grow ten feet,
   Sing song, Polly, won't you ki' me, oh?
Dey go to bed but 'taint no use,
   Sing song, Polly, won't you ki' me, oh?
Dere feet stick out for a chicken roost,
   Sing song, Polly, won't you ki' me, oh?

Dar was a frog lived in a spring,
   Sing song, Polly, won't you ki' me, oh?
He had sich a cold dat he couldn't sing,
   Sing song, Polly, won't you ki' me, oh?
I pulled him out and frowed 'im on de ground,
   Sing song, Polly, won't you ki' me, oh?
Old frog he bounced and jumped around,
   Sing song, Polly, won't you ki' me, oh?

Milk in de dairy nine days old,

    Sing song, Polly, won't you ki' me, oh?

Rats and skippers are gettin' bold,

    Sing song, Polly, won't you ki' me, oh?

A long-tail'd rat in a bucket of souse,

    Sing song, Polly, won't you ki' me, oh?

Just come from de white folks' house,

    Sing song, Polly, won't you ki' me, oh?

Chorus

Kemo kimo, dar, whar, my hi, my ho,

My rum-sti-pum-sti-did-dle

Soot bag, pidly-winkum, linkum, nip cat,

Sing song, Polly, won't you ki' me, oh?

PATRIOTIC SONGS

(*Americana*)

The following songs pertain to America's bygone days. History is hidden in their verses, and unwritten volumes between their lines.

"When in the course of human events, it becomes necessary for one people to dissolve the political bands which have connected them with another." —DECLARATION OF INDEPENDENCE.

FREE AMERICA

That seat of science, Athens,
　　And earth's proud mistress, Rome.
Where now are all their glories?
　　We scarce can find a tomb.
Then guard your rights, Americans,
　　Nor stoop to lawless sway,
Oppose, oppose, oppose, oppose,
　　For free America.

We led fair Franklin hither,
　　And, lo! the desert smiled.
A paradise of pleasure
　　Was opened to the world!
Your harvest, bold Americans,
　　No power shall snatch away!
Huzza, huzza, huzza, huzza
　　For free America.

Torn from a world of tyrants,
　　Beneath this western sky
We formed a new dominion,
　　A land of liberty.
The world shall own we're masters here;
　　Then hasten on the day:
Huzza, huzza, huzza, huzza
　　For free America.

Proud Albion bowed to Caesar,
  And numerous lords before;
To Picts, to Danes, to Normans
  And many masters more;
But we can boast, Americans,
  We've never fallen prey.
Huzza, huzza, huzza, huzza
  For free America.

God bless this maiden climate,
  And through its vast domain
May hosts of heroes cluster
  Who scorn to wear a chain,
And blast the venal sycophant
  That dares our rights betray.
Huzza, huzza, huzza, huzza
  For free America.

Lift up your heads, ye heroes,
  And swear with proud disdain
The wretch that would ensnare you
  Shall lay his snares in vain.
Should Europe empty all her force,
  We'll meet her in array
And fight and shout, and shout and fight
  For free America.

Some future day shall crown us
  The masters of the main.
Our fleets shall speak in thunder
  To England, France and Spain.
And the nations o'er the oceans spread

Shall tremble and obey
The sons, the sons, the sons, the sons
Of free America.

The above song, set to the tune of "The British Grenadiers," is ascribed to the pen of Joseph Warren, (1741-1775). An ardent American patriot, he was active in events leading up to the Revolution. Chosen second Major-General of the Massachussetts forces, he joined Putnam and Prescott at Bunker Hill as volunteer aide. He was shot and killed in the final conflict near Prescott's redoubt. Webster, in his "Bunker Hill Oration," calls him "the first great martyr in this great cause."

RED, WHITE AND BLUE

O Columbia, the gem of the ocean,
  The home of the brave and the free,
The shrine of each patriot's devotion,
  A world offers homage to thee.
Thy mandates make heroes assemble,
  When liberty's form stands in view,
Thy banners make tyrants tremble,
  When borne by the Red, White and Blue.

When war waged its wide desolation
  And threatened our land to deform,
The ark then of freedom's foundation,
  Columbia, rode safe through the storm.
With her garland of victory o'er her,
  When so proudly she bore her bold crew,
With her flag proudly floating before her,
  The boast of the Red, White and Blue.

The wine cup, the wine cup bring hither
  And fill you it up to the brim;
May the wreath they have won never wither
Nor the star of their glory grow dim!
  May the service united ne'er sever,
And hold to their colors so true!
  The Army and the Navy for ever!
Three cheers for the Red, White and Blue.

Chorus

When borne by the Red, White and Blue,
   When borne by the Red, White and Blue;
Thy banners make tyrants tremble,
   When borne by the Red, White and Blue.

". . . . our fathers brought forth on this continent a new nation, conceived in liberty, and dedicated to the proposition that all men are created equal." —LINCOLN.

THE STAR-SPANGLED BANNER

Oh! say, can you see, by the dawn's early light,
  What so proudly we hailed at the twilight's last gleaming,
Whose broad stripes and bright stars through the perilous flight,
  O'er the ramparts we watched, were so gallantly streaming?
And the rocket's red glare, the bombs bursting in air,
  Gave proof through the night that our flag was still there.
Oh, say, does that star-spangled banner yet wave
  O'er the land of the free and the home of the brave.

On the shore, dimly seen through the mists of the deep,
  Where the foe's haughty host in dread silence reposes,
What is that which the breeze, o'er the towering steep,
  As it fitfully blows, half conceals, half discloses?
Now it catches the gleam of the morning's first beam
  In full glory reflected, now shines on the stream.
'Tis the star-spangled banner: Oh, long may it wave
  O'er the land of the free, and the home of the brave.

Oh! thus be it ever when free-men shall stand
  Between their loved homes and wild war's desolation.
Blest with victory and peace, may the heaven-rescued land
  Praise the power that hath made and preserved us a nation.
Then conquer we must, when our cause it is just,
  And this be our motto, "In God is our trust!"
And the star-spangled banner in triumph shall wave
  O'er the land of the free and the home of the brave.

"Now we are engaged in a great civil war; testing whether that nation, or any nation so conceived and so dedicated, can long endure." —LINCOLN.

THE BATTLE CRY OF FREEDOM

Yes, we'll rally round the flag, boys, we'll rally once again,
    Shouting the battle cry of Freedom,
We will rally from the hillside, we'll gather from the plain,
    Shouting the battle cry of Freedom.

We are springing to the call of our brothers gone before,
    Shouting the battle cry of Freedom.
And we'll fill the vacant ranks with a million freemen more,
    Shouting the battle cry of Freedom.

We will welcome to our numbers the loyal true and brave,
    Shouting the battle cry of Freedom.
And although they may be poor, not a man shall be a slave.
    Shouting the battle cry of Freedom.

So we're springing to the call from the East and from the West,
    Shouting the battle cry of Freedom.
And we'll hurl the rebel crew from the land we love the best
    Shouting the battle cry of Freedom.

Chorus

The Union forever, Hurrah boys, Hurrah!
Down with the traitor, up with the star;
While we rally round the flag, boys, rally once again,
Shouting the battle cry of Freedom.

THE BONNIE BLUE FLAG

We are a band of brothers, and native to the soil,
    Fighting for the property we gained by honest toil;
And when our rights were threatened, the cry rose near and far,
    Hurrah for the Bonnie Blue Flag, that bears a Single Star.

As long as the old Union was faithful to her trust,
    Like friends and like brothers, kind were we and just;
But now, when Northern treachery attempts our rights to mar,
    We hoist on high the Bonnie Blue Flag, that bears a Single Star.

First, gallant South Carolina nobly made the stand;
    Then came Alabama, who took her by the hand,
Next, quickly Mississippi, Georgia and Florida,
    All raised on high the Bonnie Blue Flag that bears a Single Star.

Ye men of valor, gather round the Banner of the Right,
    Texas and fair Louisiana join us in the fight.
Davis, our loved President, and Stephens, statesman rare,
    Now rally round the Bonnie Blue Flag that bears a Single Star.

And here's to brave Virginia! the Old Dominion State
    With the young Confederacy at length has linked her fate.
Impelled by her example, now other states prepare
    To hoist on high the Bonnie Blue Flag that bears a Single Star.

Then here's to our Confederacy, strong we are and brave,
    Like patriots of old, we'll fight our heritage to save.
And rather than submit to shame, to die we would prefer,
    So cheer for the Bonnie Blue Flag that bears a Single Star.

Then cheer, boys, cheer, raise the joyous shout,

For Arkansas and North Carolina now have both gone out.
And let another rousing cheer for Tennessee be given —
The Single Star of the Bonnie Blue Flag has grown to be Eleven.

Chorus

Hurrah! Hurrah! for Southern Rights, hurrah!
Hurrah! for the Bonnie Blue Flag, that bears a Single Star.

Final Chorus

Hurrah! Hurrah! for Southern Rights, hurrah!
Hurrah! for the Bonnie Blue Flag has gained the eleventh Star.

SHERMAN'S MARCH TO THE SEA

Our camp-fires shone bright on the mountains
  That frowned on the river below,
While we stood by our guns, in the morning,
  And eagerly watched for the foe,
When a rider came out from the darkness
  That hung over mountain and tree,
And shouted, "Boys, up! and be ready!
  For, Sherman will march to the sea!"

Then cheer upon cheer for bold Sherman
  Went up from each valley and glen,
And the bugles re-echoed the music
  That came from the lips of the men.
For we knew that the stars on our banner
  More bright in their splendor would be,
And that blessings from North-Land would greet us,
  When Sherman marched down to the sea!

Then, forward! boys, forward to battle!
  We marched on our wearisome way,
And we stormed the wild hills of Resacs —
  God bless those that fell on that day!
Then Kenesaw, dark in its glory,
  Frowned down on the flag of the free,
But the East and the West bore our standards,
  And Sherman marched down to the sea!

Still onward we pressed, till our banners
   Swept out from Atlanta's grim walls,
And the blood of the patriot dampened
   The soil where the traitor's flag falls;
But we paused not to weep for the fallen
   Who slept by each river and tree;
Yet we twined them a wreath of the laurel,
   As Sherman marched down to the sea!

Proud, proud was our army, that morning,
   That stood where the pine proudly towers,
When Sherman said, "Boys, you are weary,
   This day, fair Savannah is ours!"
Then sung we a song for our Chieftain,
   That echoed o'er river and lea,
And the stars on our banner shone brighter
   When Sherman marched down to the sea!

MARCHING THROUGH GEORGIA

Bring the good bugle, boys, we'll sing another song —
  Sing it with a spirit that will start the world along —
Sing it as we used to sing it, fifty thousand strong,
  While we were marching through Georgia.

How the darkies shouted when they heard the joyful sound;
  How the turkeys gobbled which our Commissary found;
How the sweet potatoes even started from the ground,
  While we were marching through Georgia.

Yes, and there were Union men who wept with joyful tears,
  When they saw the honored flag they had not seen for years;
Hardly could they be restrained from breaking forth in cheers,
  While we were marching through Georgia.

Sherman's dashing Yankee boys will never reach the coast;
  So the saucy Rebels said — and 'twas a handsome boast;
Had they not forgot, alas! to reckon with the host,
  While we were marching through Georgia.

So we made a thoroughfare for Freedom and her train,
  Sixty miles in latitude, three hundred to the main;
Treason fled before us, for resistance was in vain,
  While we were marching through Georgia.

Chorus

  Hurrah! hurrah! we bring the jubilee!
  Hurrah! hurrah! the flag that makes you free!
  So we sang the chorus from Atlanta to the sea,
  While we were marching through Georgia.

STONEWALL'S REQUIEM

The muffled drum is beating, there's a sad and solemn tread,
   Our Banner's draped in mourning as it shrouds "the illustrious
                                    [dead."
Proud forms are bent with sorrow and all Southern hearts are sore,
   The hero now is sleeping — noble Stonewall is no more.
'Mid the rattling of the muskets and the cannon's thunderous roar,
   He stained the field of glory with his brave life's precious gore,
And though our flag waved proudly — we were victors ere sunset,
   The gallant deeds of Chancelorsville will mingle with regret.

They've borne him to an honored grave, the laurel crowns his brow,
   By hallowed James' silent wave He's sweetly sleeping now.
Virginia to the South is dear, she holds a sacred trust,
   Our fallen braves from far and near are covered with her dust.
She shrines the spot where now is laid the bravest of them all,
   The martyr of our country's cause, our idolized Stonewall.
But though his spirit's wafted to the happy realms above,
   His name shall live forever linked with reverence and love.

TENTING ON THE OLD CAMP-GROUND

We're tenting tonight on the old camp-ground, give us a song to
    cheer
Our weary hearts, a song of home, and friends we love so dear.

Chorus

> Many are the hearts that are weary tonight,
>   Wishing for the war to cease.
> Many are the hearts looking for the right,
>   To see the dawn of peace.
> Tenting tonight, tenting tonight,
>   Tenting on the old camp-ground.

We've been tenting, tonight, on the old camp-ground, thinking of
    the days gone by,
Of the loved ones at home, that gave us the hand, and the tears that
    said, "Good-bye!"

We are tired of war on the old camp-ground, many are dead and
    gone,
Of the brave and true who've left their homes; others have been
    wounded long.

We've been fighting today on the old camp-ground; many are
    lying near —
Some are dead, and some are dying — many are in tears!

Chorus

> Many are the hearts that are weary tonight,
>   Wishing for the war to cease.
> Many are the hearts looking for the right,
>   To see the dawn of peace.
> Dying tonight, dying tonight,
>   Dying on the old camp-ground.

"United we stand." E pluribus unum statu quo ante bellum.

MY COUNTRY, 'TIS OF THEE
(America)

My country, 'tis of thee,
Sweet land of liberty,
    Of thee I sing.
Land where my fathers died,
Land of the pilgrim's pride,
From every mountain side,
    Let freedom ring.

My native country, thee,
Land of the noble free,
    Thy name I love.
I love thy rocks and rills,
Thy woods and templed hills;
My heart with rapture thrills
    Like that above.

Let music swell the breeze,
And ring from all the trees,
    Sweet freedom's song.
Let mortal tongues awake,
Let all that breathe partake,
Let rocks their silence break,
    The sound prolong.

Our father's God, to thee,
Author of liberty,
  To thee I sing.
Long may our land be bright

With freedom's holy light;
Protect us by thy might
  Great God, our King.

INDEX

TO

TRADITIONAL MUSIC OF AMERICA

INDEX

ACCOMPANIMENTS

SQUARE DANCE MUSIC

Quadrilles and Fiddle Tunes

INDEX

474

INDEX

INDEX

INDEX

477

INDEX

INDEX

INDEX